Communism

Communism

FOURTH EDITION

Alfred G. Meyer
University of Michigan

RANDOM HOUSE  NEW YORK

Fourth Edition

987654321

Copyright © 1960, 1962, 1967, 1984 by Random House, Inc.

Library of Congress Cataloging in Publication Data

Meyer, Alfred G.
  Communism.

  Bibliography: p.
  Includes index.
  1. Communism. 2. Communism—Soviet Union. I. Title.
HX40.M43 1984   335.43   83–11188
ISBN 0-394-33163-X

Manufactured in the United States of America

Preface to the Fourth Edition

Fifteen years is a long time in the history of revolutions, and the changes to be recorded since this book was last revised are numerous and deep.

I have made many minor additions and deletions, have condensed and rearranged Chapters 5 through 8, and have integrated a new chapter. Chapters 10 and 11 have been expanded considerably. I have brought the notes and the bibliography up-to-date, but that task is elusive: The literature in the field of communist studies grows so rapidly that no scholar, even if he or she had no other obligations, would be able to keep up with it.

I have tried to eliminate sexism from my language by saying *person* or *human being* where formerly I said *man*. I have also felt free to refer to the founding fathers of communism either as "Marx and Engels" or as "Engels and Marx"; they were genuine partners, even though Engels often belittled his own role, and, in any event, we ought not to allow our language to turn into a litany of fixed formulations, for frozen language leads to frozen thought.

I want to express my appreciation to Patricia Willacker for her excellent work in helping me edit the manuscript for the present edition.

Alfred G. Meyer

Preface to the Third Edition

Developments in the communist world have wrought changes far more profound and rapid than any Western social scientist would have dared predict a few years ago. To account for these changes, I have undertaken a comparatively thorough revision of this book. In adding an account of most recent transformations of the communist world, I have also made minor corrections in chapters that remained relatively unchanged. Moreover, parts of the previous book were rearranged—a chapter was eliminated, others were merged—for the sake of achieving a more logical or cohesive presentation.

With regard to one sentiment expressed in the preface to the first two editions I have had second thoughts: In professing my intention to show some moral or political detachment, I had hoped to view communism outside of a narrow cold war perspective and thus to avoid some of the stereotypes fostered in our minds by the cold war. It would be foolish, however, to pretend that I am without values or biases. Indeed, the present book, like its previous versions, will show that my general attitude toward communism is as critical as is my attitude toward other political and social systems, including my own. To zealots on both sides, I know, my attitude is objectionable, and they are not likely to approve of this book.

I am grateful to Adam Ulam for suggesting some of the changes to be made. My special thanks go to Anne Dyer Murphy, an exceedingly competent editor, and a friend.

Alfred G. Meyer

Preface to the First and Second Editions

This introduction to communism in its various guises and functions is intended for a broad public of advanced and beginning students, policy makers, and the proverbial intelligent reader—for anyone, in short, who wants to study the subject with a minimum of political passion. I stress my effort to achieve political detachment because I feel that much of what the general public reads about communism so caters to an attitude of disapproval that it can enlighten no one.

Some may feel that the essay style I have chosen does not suit the purposes of the book, but I believe that authors must reveal themselves even when endeavoring to outline their subject and the principal controversies about it. I have tried to counteract personal interpretation by guiding the reader, at every major step, to the ample literature in this field.

I have profited from comments by Samuel Krislov, Archibald Singham, and Donald Urquidi, who read brief sections of the manuscript. Some of my statements would have been different or would not have been made prior to my 1958 trip to the USSR and Poland. For this enlightening travel I am grateful to the Inter-University Travel Grant Committee. To the administration of Michigan State University I owe thanks for releasing me from teaching for a quarter so that I could complete the manuscript. My special gratitude goes to Charles D. Lieber, of Random House, who encouraged me to write this study, and to Mrs. Leonore C. Hauck, of the same firm.

Alfred G. Meyer

Contents

Communism

CHAPTER 1

Introduction

The word "communism" means different things to different people, and its meaning may change from time to time. To some political leaders in colonial or dependent nations it may imply revolt against white rule, liberation from colonialism, and rapid industrialization, aided by Soviet, Chinese, Cuban, or German money, goods, or advice. To workers in some Western European countries, from Italy to Finland, it may imply defense of lower-class interests and sharp criticism of American foreign policy, if not sympathy with the Russians, the Chinese, or at least the struggle against apartheid. Many a Western intellectual will regard it as a utopian ideal tarnished by inhuman practices. To the police it is an international conspiracy of power-mad criminals. To the citizens of any socialist country, the word connotes, in one sense, a meaningful goal their society is striving to attain within the foreseeable future and, in a broader sense, their country's entire way of life, with its rewards and its hardships. Communism means an ideal, a political movement, a method of analysis, and a way of life. It may even mean a set of attitudes that psychologists might be able to reduce to a syndrome of personality traits. Some people regard it as the product and property of Western civilization, while others see it primarily as an anti-Western revolt, or as a denial of all Western values and traditions.

Obviously, communism is protean; its meaning depends on time and place, circumstance, and on the point of view of the observer. Even its articulate ethos, Marxist theory, clothes itself in garbs of many hues. The theory itself distinguishes different levels of understanding and tries, accordingly, to speak to different

1

publics. It also views reality on different levels of concreteness or abstraction, so that it takes long-, short-, and intermediate-range views of the setting, the goals, and the strategies of the communist movement. Outsiders, meanwhile, note the tendency toward the development of an esoteric communist language that, some maintain, serves as a complicated code only the initiates know how to decipher.

Because the present study is to serve as a general introduction to the subject, I am obliged to approach it eclectically, as perhaps any political phenomenon ought to be approached, if adequate understanding is to be gained. In viewing communism in its various aspects, we shall pay particular attention to a number of problems that run through these various facets of our subject: The element of change—what transformations have communist ideas and practices undergone from the time of Marx? The element of diversity—what different schools of communism have arisen and which have survived? How important are the differences between communism in Europe and communism in Central America, between communist revolutionaries and communist government officials? Is it meaningful to call these various political forces by the same name? Finally, we shall try to assess the nature of the much-discussed ''challenge'' of communism. Should communism be regarded as a threat to Western civilization, and, if so, in what way is it a threat? Is communism likely to gain adherents and make converts in the years and decades to come? If so, what makes it attractive? What elements in it appeal to people not yet committed to it?

I shall start by presenting the theory of communism, and perhaps this requires justification, because many scholars would dismiss communist theory as irrelevant. They would describe communist doctrine as a grab bag of ideas cynically used by Machiavellian manipulators at the head of communist governments and parties to justify whatever policies they choose to adopt while seeking to gain or maintain power for its own sake. I do not agree with those writers who would derive all actions of communist parties or governments from Marxist ideology. But neither is it entirely true, as many other scholars claim, that the ''means have eaten up the ends.'' To be sure, although communism gives a great deal of emphasis to the final goal in its theories, its short-range planning and actions seem to be guided by the revisionist principle that the end is nothing, the means everything. Yet these means were derived from the ends. As Richard Lowenthal correctly says, there can be no *Realpolitik* without ideological preconceptions.* The theory, moreover, is more than a set of goals. It is also a method of analysis, and it has remained a methodological gridwork through which its initiates view and explain reality. Finally, communism still is a definable state of mind, and the attitudes composing it are also derived in part from Marxism.

In short, communist theory is more than rationalization. The thoughts and actions of communist leaders are determined in significant measure by the intellectual heritage of Marx, Lenin, Stalin, and others. But even if this were not so, the fact remains that their ideology remains one of the strongest forces active in the world today. And therefore it must be studied by anyone trying to understand contemporary history.

However, we cannot hope to understand the strength—and the weaknesses—of communist ideas without examining communism as a system of government, a way of life, and an active political movement. Nor can we hope to grasp the meaning of communist ideas without studying the historical and political context within which they were shaped and changed. We shall therefore have to discuss several communist societies now existing in the world. We must be aware that these societies and the governments managing them have been subject to change. Hence it will be necessary to discuss, at least cursorily, typical phases of communist rule, which may at times be as different from each other as present-day Soviet Russia is from present-day America or even from present-day China, and also the various phases of the policies of the international communist movement.

The resulting image will be complex and, for those who like easy generalizations, unsatisfactory. In order to provide a framework for all the loose pieces we shall have in our hands—and at the risk of oversimplification—let me suggest one such generalization: It seems to me that twentieth-century communism, in all its variations, can be understood to some extent if we regard it as our age's equivalent to seventeenth-century Puritanism (which includes as many varying phenomena as

*"Ideology and Power Politics: A Symposium," *Problems of Communism*, VII, No. 2 (March–April 1958), pp. 10–35.

communism).* To support this suggestion, let me draw attention to some of the innumerable parallels that can be drawn between the two phenomena.

Puritanism and communism share a number of important broad ideas and political goals. Both claimed to strive for liberty and against tyranny, even though in the name of liberty both set up starkly autocratic regimes. Both claimed to fight for equality and human brotherhood and against the privileges or abuses of ruling classes and hierarchies; yet both set up societies marked by gross inequalities of reward, and in their ideologies they found justification for such inequalities. Both claimed overriding justification—be it God's will or historical inevitability—for destroying institutions they regarded as artificial, unnatural, or imposed. Both, finally, claimed that their aim was to carry out the ideals of revolutions that had preceded them by a century or more. The Puritans gave themselves their name because their avowed aim was to fulfill, or purify, the Reformation; whereas communism promises to fulfill the broken promises of the French Revolution.

Puritanism as well as communism are theories of salvation and damnation, incorporating the notion of inevitability (predestination). Both movements fought (or fight) for an invincible cause, guided and strengthened by a Holy Writ that played a central role in shaping the minds of entire generations. Both the Puritans and the communists are fully convinced that "objective reality" or "God's will" can be understood through careful study of the scriptures. Both movements developed their thought into complicated and involved systems of ideas that include theories of history, human nature, society, and the entire universe, and provide standards for behavior, including a theory of leadership and obedience. In both cases, moreover, the revolutionary zeal of educated speakers appealed to broad strata of the lower, underprivileged classes, who were exhorted to despise and destroy the prevailing authorities. Yet, once the leaders had installed themselves in power, that same zeal caused them to impose intolerable conditions and superhuman standards of performance on the citizens.

In both Puritanism and communism we have, I think, cases of

*Similarities can also be seen between communism and later forms of Puritanism, for instance, Victorianism.

liberational movements gone sour and pessimistic, movements that are therefore marked by strange ambivalences in judgment and contradictions in both goals and methods. For both, an intellectual point of departure is the belief in the sovereignty of the autonomous human personality; in one case it is the individual in a direct relationship to his or her God; in the other case it is the proletariat in its crucial role in history. But in both cases serious doubt has arisen. For the Puritans, this implied a renewed emphasis on original sin; for the communists beginning with Lenin, the belief that the working class by itself could never attain consciousness. In both movements, the practical consequence was that the earlier democratic conception that human beings would freely and spontaneously choose the road to (heavenly or earthly) salvation gave way to the idea that the elect, the vanguard, the chosen few would have to force the masses into salvation. Yet, while the individual (or the class) is regarded as weak and untrustworthy, while the movement has little faith in the autonomous personality, it still burdens the individual with grave responsibility for his or her actions and thoughts. Distrust in human nature or an emphasis on original sin is accompanied by the attempt to make every person into a fully rational being or into a saint, while the gloomy realization that this task might be impossible drives the movement to manipulation, coercion, and terror, carried out in both cases by an organization of the elect that coopts its members, while going through the motions of elections or other democratic procedures. In organization, in procedure, in the purges they carried out, and in their actual and pretended relationship to government authorities (once a Puritan or communist government has been created), the organization of the elect and the Communist party bear striking resemblances to each other.

The underlying pessimism is expressed in the conviction that Satan (or capitalism) will surely defeat the cause of righteousness if the movement relents for but a little moment in its zealous devotion to the dogma, in its intolerance of deviation and laxness. Indeed, the devil lurks behind the most angelic masks, and both the Puritan and the communist are therefore witch hunters, who tend to explain untoward developments by the weakest of all social theories—the conspiratorial theory. At the basis of the deep pessimism that characterizes both Puritanism and communism is, perhaps, the fact that both these revolutionary movements were only partly successful, that they were forced to *coexist* with their enemy. Theoretically, neither movement was prepared for prolonged coexistence during which it might be obliged to have friendly or at least civil relations with the enemy. Both were profoundly disturbed by the experience.

Coexistence fortified the tendency of both Puritans and communists to see everything in black and white and to divide the human race into friends and enemies, recognizing no shadings or positions in between truth and falsehood. Both are totalitarian in that they seek to infuse every realm of human endeavor with the spirit of their movement. Everything a person may do has religious (or political) significance. No pursuits are undertaken for their own sake but must be given the spirit of *partiinost'*.* Precisely because the movements are forced to accommodate "temporarily" to coexistence with the foe, they must banish all thoughts of lasting or meaningful accommodation. Because of this pessimism and the resulting ambivalence, the urge to cleanse out what is rotten and wrong is given a note of frantic urgency. Every action counts. Everything that is done is decisive.

Despite the otherworldly orientation of the Puritans and the lofty humanism of communist doctrine, both movements must be characterized as intensely materialistic and secular. The principal orientation of both can be said to be *accumulation*, that is, economic growth. And just as the American Puritans went forth into the wilderness to carry civilization to the aborigines, so communism is the pioneer movement that in our century seeks to civilize (in the material sense) the underdeveloped nations, that aims to bring social mobility and the spirit of work to indolent cultures. There is about both movements the same missionary spirit, the same desire to liberate all humanity from evil and sloth.

In both cases, finally, this mission is carried out with an almost inhuman earnestness, with a complete lack of a sense of humor, and a stern intolerance of frivolity and hedonism. The drabness of Soviet towns, the stark utilitarianism of Chinese communist garments, the primness of Soviet sex morality are as Puritan as they could be and remind us vividly of the pictures we have seen of America in the days of the Western pioneers. In both cases, the

*For an explanation of this term, see pp. 116–117.

individual is to be serious, thrifty, and single-mindedly devoted to the goal of accumulating wealth.

However, Soviet towns are not longer quite so drab. High heels and polka dot dresses now cover the bodies of middle-class women in the USSR; jeans and college sweatshirts now appear on nonconformist youngsters in the larger cities. Even in China, the revolutionary uniform worn by all during the reign of Mao is giving way to more cheerful clothing. These changes in fashion symbolize the fact that harsh puritanical dictatorship cannot sustain itself indefinitely. The strains, such as the human cost of terror and thought control, become excessive. To ease the strain and maintain the societies they created, both the USSR and China ultimately transformed themselves, however gradually, into more pluralistic and open societies. Their centralized control was mitigated by citizen participation, a participation encouraged not only by the threats of punishment but also by the promise of rewards.

In the end, Puritanism softened and gave way to less severe forms of social organization. There are indications that similar processes have for a long time been going on in contemporary communist regimes. This will be discussed in later chapters of this book.

The similarities between communism and Puritanism that I have pointed out have been noticed by previous observers.* But they deserve mention nevertheless because I think that the comparison gives us a rather unusual view of communism, an angle of vision that might help to explain features and relationships that might otherwise remain puzzles. In addition, I find the *déjà-vu* feeling this perspective gives me a bit reassuring, for the comparison suggests that communism might not be as novel, as strange, or as alien to Western traditions as it appears to most of us and as many of its adherents would like to make it seem. At the same time, as a decidedly antipuritan person, I find that this view adds support to the antipathy I feel toward various features in the development of communism.

This, with minor modifications, is the way I introduced the

---

*See Harold J. Laski, *Reflections on the Revolution of Our Time* (New York, 1943), pp. 73–75; Eduard Bernstein, *Cromwell and Communism: Socialism and Democracy in the Great English Revolution* (London, 1930), pp. 26–30; and Leon Trotsky, *Whither England?* (New York, 1925), pp. 60–61 and *passim*.

subject of the book in previous editions. I am not sure whether I would write it that way today. At the least, I would suggest another analogy. Instead of comparing twentieth-century communism with seventeenth-century Puritanism, I would be tempted to bring out those similarities between modern communism and the earliest stirrings of Christianity in the Roman Empire—a comparison that already fascinated Friedrich Engels. Among other things, Christianity originated as a radical alternative to the day's politics. It was first embraced as a message of delivery by the poor, by the enslaved, and by upper-class women. It was then seized on by the "backward" nations at the fringes of the Empire—the Roman equivalent of what we call the Third World. It was a movement of the exploited, the deprived, and the underdeveloped, and it was fiercely resisted by the wealthy, the powerful, and the educated. In the end Christianity won. However, once in power, it turned into yet another authoritarian hierarchy ruling with murderous fanaticism. Like communism, the impact of Christianity and its ideas are still felt everywhere today.

Let us then analyze the growth, the ideas, and the way of life of communism, beginning with the writings of Karl Marx and Friedrich Engels. Although I am beginning with an exposition of Marxist doctrine, I do not wish to imply the existence of a causal chain from doctrine to institutions. There is a much more complicated reciprocal relationship between ideas and politics, and at all its stages of development the doctrine itself can be understood only as a response to real social problems. Hence an introduction to Marxist theories should properly begin with the Industrial Revolution, the French Revolution, and the social and political problems resulting from both.

CHAPTER 2

The Ideas of
Marx and Engels

The emergence of nineteenth-century industrial society brought massive social dislocation and misery. Technological progress made entire classes of small producers and distributors obsolete, impoverished them, degraded them on the social scale, and forced them into the burgeoning cities, where unspeakable working and living conditions awaited them. Socialism as a mass movement began as the rebellion of the working class against their misery. Sporadic, almost aimless uprisings, such as those of the weavers in Silesia, the machine-wrecking Luddites in England, or the numerous working-class rebellions of 1848, mark the beginnings of the socialist movement. As a political theory, it developed when the workers' lot was contrasted with the liberal rhetoric prevailing at the time. Its point of departure was the assertion that the ideals of the American and French revolutions—liberty, equality, fraternity, and the right to a human existence—had been betrayed, and that the promise of these revolutions could be fulfilled only if political rights were matched by social and economic equality, by wiping out the difference between rich and poor. Beyond this, we cannot generalize about advocates or theorists of socialism. They have differed sharply not only over the definition of the kind of society that would rectify these ills but even more over the methods that would bring it into existence. They have included atheists and believers, pacifists and terrorists, criminals and saints, authoritarians and anarchists, and all shadings in between. The variety of socialist schools that has developed in the last 170 years is made clear to us when we realize that, in the vague sense I have given to the word, almost everyone today is a socialist or has accepted socialist ideals.*

Communism regards itself as the legitimate heir of all that is valid and good in the socialist tradition. It looks on the working-class revolts of the early nineteenth century as the beginnings of its own movement and regards the first socialists, beginning with Gracchus Babeuf, as precursors of its most honored prophets, Marx and Engels (who, incidentally, preferred to call themselves communists rather than socialists, in order to emphasize their disagreements with other socialists).

The precursors of Marx and Engels are often referred to as "utopian socialists." This term was used by the Marxists themselves in criticism of both the detailed descriptions of the coming socialist society that earlier theorists had given and their failure to indicate how these societies might be brought into existence. In contrast, Engels and Marx regarded their communism as scientific socialism. They claimed to have proven that the coming of socialism was inevitable, and their entire doctrine is an attempt to support this assertion. Marxism can therefore be defined as that school of socialism that seeks to prove that socialism is inevitable.

As we shall see a little later, Marxists support this assertion partly by moral argument: Capitalism so degrades individuals, so frustrates their potentialities for creative development, that life under it is hell on earth, a mockery of all the ethical commands associated with the Christian-liberal tradition. But men and women still retain their innate ability to shape a good life for themselves through socialism.

Engels and Marx, however, denied that they were moral philosophers or prophets preaching reform to an evil society. When they asserted the inevitability of socialism, they used the word "inevitable" in a descriptive (or, as they would have put it, scientific) sense. The existing system, they thought, simply could

---

*Descriptions of the conditions of the working class in early capitalism abound not only in Marxist literature, beginning with Engels' *The Condition of the Working Class in England* (New York, 1958) and Marx's *Capital*, but are more familiar to us through the novels of Dickens, Victor Hugo, and others. For a more recent description of similar conditions in the United States, see Oscar Handlin, *The Uprooted* (Boston, 1951); E.P. Thompson, *The Making of the English Working Class* (London, 1963); and Steven Marcus, *Engels, Manchester, and the Working Class* (New York, 1974).

not last, and all the conditions necessary for the birth of socialism had come into being. The core of this doctrine was and remains the Marxist description of capitalism and the "laws" governing it—that is, the manner in which the system functioned. According to these laws, capitalism was well suited to ensure economic growth in the early industrial age, and Marx therefore assigns the most important place to capitalism among the stages in the march of human progress. No social philosopher, perhaps, has rivaled the songs of praise that Marx and Engels sang to capitalism in their *Communist Manifesto.* At the same time, however, Marxism asserts that the same laws that made capitalism advance the progress of the human race would bring misery, chaos, crisis, and final breakdown to the mature capitalist society. Institutions, habits, and intellectual traditions that had once strengthened the system would burden and fetter it intolerably and would hasten its collapse.

The fundamental law governing the Marxist model of capitalism is that of the market. In basing his analysis on this law, Marx follows in the footsteps of Adam Smith and other "classical" economists. He differs from them on several counts. For one thing, he places market economies into historical perspective by pointing out that they were preceded by different systems. There are societies in which people produce only to satisfy their immediate needs or those of their masters. Under capitalism, however, they produce marketable commodities, and all their economic activity is guided, even dictated, by the market. Another assertion distinguishing Marxism from classical economic theories is that under capitalism the labor power of the "immediate producers"—the workers—is bought and sold as if it were a commodity. Therefore, the very lives of people who are compelled to work for a living are subject to the laws of the market. Life has become a market place, with human work, human emotions, human spirit bought and sold as a commodity.

To Marx, this transformation of human labor power into a commodity is the specific feature that distinguishes capitalism from all other market economies and therefore from all other modes of production as well. Since, according to Marx, human labor is the only creative force, its subjection to the laws of the market introduced into that market a curious element both constructive and disruptive: a commodity that, through the creation of values, could not only reproduce itself but could create far more than its own market value.

Before we pursue this, we must note one other line of argument connected with the definition of capitalism as that mode of production in which human labor power has become a commodity. I have in mind the attempt Marx and Engels made to show beyond any doubt that capitalism was an exploitative system. To do so, they again followed in the footsteps of classical economics by incorporating in their market theory a theory of value. Most Western economists today do not take the Marxist theory of value seriously and tend to regard the very notion of value as meaningless. They have usually failed to see, however, the crucial role that the Marxist theory of value plays, not as a concept in economic analysis, but as a description of *social* relationships in a market economy. Of particular significance here is the relationship between capitalist and worker, because, on the basis of his particular definition of value and the classical laws of the market, Marx could argue that the workers, selling their labor power at its true value, were nevertheless cheated out of a portion of what their labor produced.

From the concept of human labor as a commodity producing surplus value and from the relationship of this human commodity to the "dead" commodities (materials, machines, and so forth) used in production, Marx derived additional laws governing both the growth and collapse of capitalism. These laws describe capitalism as a system compelled by its inner dynamic to accumulate capital at an ever-increasing rate and to invest it in new enterprises even though a constantly falling rate of profit made investment more and more difficult. The force of these laws was further seen to drive increasing numbers of capitalists to their ruin, swelling the ranks of the propertyless proletariat. Fiercely competing with each other, the workers would drive down the market value of human labor power, creating additional misery for the proletariat. Capitalism was therefore a system that had, through technological and social progress, led humanity to the threshold of an era in which the material needs of all humanity could be filled, if only the technological achievements could be used rationally. But the laws governing capitalist production had caused the system to become entangled in hopeless difficulties: a free-enterprise system in which all individuals operated blindly and helplessly; a productive capacity that could not be used; surplus human beings who could not be employed; surplus commodities that could neither be sold nor given away, even while poverty was increasing.

These and similar problems, Marx and Engels believed, capitalism could not possibly solve without destroying itself. Inevitably, therefore, the system would collapse, and socialism would rise from the ruins. This death and rebirth of society would take the form of a revolution in which the proletariat would expropriate the capitalists and reorganize the economy on completely different, and rational, principles. Society would then be able to satisfy all people's material needs. Inequality and exploitation would be abolished. Oppressive institutions and inhuman behavior would become superfluous and dysfunctional and would wither away. As a matter of fact, all institutions, habits, traditions, beliefs, behavior patterns, and the like, now confining and constraining human beings and preventing them from freely being themselves, would become superfluous. Having become fully rational, all human beings would also become convinced that their own private interests could be satisfied only if they were identified with the interests of all. We would become like brothers and sisters; (Marx and Engels implicitly included women in their discussions of social issues, but they took very little pain to stress their inclusion). People's relations with each other would be free and easy and spontaneous. This belief in the coming brotherhood (and sisterhood) led many communists in the years immediately following the Russian Revolution to believe that law courts and the police, money and wages, sexual morals and the institution of the monogamous family, and many other elements of social life would disappear in the very near future.

Crucial to this vision of inevitability was the belief that the proletariat would be equipped to destroy the old and erect the new. And, in Marxist theory, the working class is indeed endowed with education, rationality, discipline, organization, and other qualities that, taken together, transform them into a Chosen People who will lead humanity into an earthly Promised Land.

This image of the proletariat and the society within which it exists is based on several important assumptions. There is, first, Marx's insistence that social studies are a science. To use his and Hegel's terminology: History proceeds in accordance to laws, *gesetzmässig*, and because of this it can be understood by people. This belief in our ability to understand history is based, in turn, on the axiom that we are rational and therefore potentially free, freedom being defined as the ability to shape one's destiny and to develop one's inherent potentialities to the fullest extent.

The question that arises at once is one that Rousseau posed in the first page of his *Social Contract*: If human beings are free, why are they everywhere in chains? In the same spirit, Marx might have asked why our fate is not freely made by us but is determined by our environment, even though we are rational. Rousseau's answer is that civilization corrupted and enslaved human beings. Marx's reply is rather similar. In his theory, a human is the animal that *produces*—which means that humans strive intelligently and purposively to master the forces and resources of nature. Except on the most primitive level, however, production is an organized activity, not of individuals, but of societies, which in conformity with their technological and scientific achievements develop social structures and institutions as a framework or machinery for carrying out the activity of production. For Marx, the history of humanity is the development of different modes of production, that is, of different types of social structures, from primitive and inefficient to highly complex and efficient ones, all of which must be seen primarily as machineries designed to master the forces of nature and to ensure our survival and comfort.

The most important principle of social structuring, in Marx's theory, is the class structure. Marxism maintains that the division of labor in all societies has led to the development of classes, the different classes being defined by their relations to the essential means of production. And, since control over these means of production confers decisive power over the entire community, the class that wields such control is not only playing a different role in the economy, it also plays a different political role by becoming the ruling class.

Marxism contains a theory of lag: Although a correspondence can be traced between class structure and technology and general mode of production, these productive forces are seen as developing on and on while the production relations show tendencies toward becoming rigid and self-perpetuating. Human progress is conceived as proceeding at varying speeds. New production relations win over older, and "lower," forces. A new ruling class controlling these new forces establishes itself and builds social institutions corresponding to the new mode of production. Once in power, however, the new ruling class seeks to perpetuate its rule even if it is made obsolete and superfluous by further economic progress. The class structure becomes a drag on further progress. The superstructure of institutions, ideologies, and habits, which once was part of the forces of progress, now paralyzes further development. The productive forces and production relations are in conflict with each other. People's past actions dominate the present generation. They do so all the more easily because people, according to Marx, are not, as a rule, aware of their state of subjection to the forces of the past. They believe they are masters of their fate even while they have only a false consciousness of the relationships that constitute the mainspring of their respective societies. This false consciousness, which Marx called ideology, enables them to live in unjust and moribund societies. It also prevents them from seeing the impending doom of these societies.

Thus our freedom is only potential. But Engels and Marx believed that it could be realized. All their doctrine is based on a yearning for freedom and on the assumption that history is continual progress in the realization of freedom, a movement toward a society worthy of the human race. This vision of progress is related to a humanist ethic based on the principle that "man, for man, is the highest being," and that therefore everything that pains or degrades us must be abolished. Like all socialists, Marx and Engels denounced the free-enterprise system for having betrayed liberal values. Unlike some of them, however, they went further and criticized *all* societies, past and present, for having betrayed basic human values. Their doctrine calls for the most radical criticism of social institutions. Just as Rousseau and the romantics had contended that civilization is evil and spoils human nature, so Marx and Engels held that human relationships in civilized society—torn as it is by class conflict—are false, evil, unworthy and that, in such a society, humans are *alienated* from nature, their fellow humans, and even themselves. Class societies dehumanize humanity. Their moral indignation at such alienation pervades all their writings, especially those that preceded their economic analysis of capitalism. They were radical humanists before they became Marxists.

In contrast, however, to present-day critics of mass culture and the bureaucratic society, Marx and Engels were optimists. As a matter of fact, their doctrine is the last example of the great optimistic ideologies that have succeeded each other in the Western tradition; it is, in that sense, the direct heir of liberalism.

This optimism is based on the idea that humanity can solve all its problems without divine assistance, because of its essentially rational nature. The Marxist view of human nature is Promethean; it sees human beings as capable, like Prometheus, of defying the gods and stealing their fire to provide themselves with the warmth of material comfort and the light of knowledge. Marxism is an arrogant ideology, and religious thinkers in our day often condemn it as a "secular religion." In their view humanity is afflicted with original sin and therefore forever unable to solve all its problems. They regard the intention to create the good life on this earth as presumptuous and blasphemous, and they point out that the attempt to carry out this intention, condemned in advance to failure, must lead to totalitarian tyranny.*

Marx and Engels, however, had no such fears. To be sure, they foresaw and even welcomed a period of violence and dictatorship that would link capitalism with communism. Meaningful change, in their eyes, could not but take the form of revolution. No ruling class, they thought, had ever given up or would ever give up its power without a desperate struggle. Nor could the change from one mode of production to another proceed without the old superstructure of institutions and beliefs being smashed. History, they held, progresses in leaps; where certain features lag behind the development of the means of production, there must be sharp breaks with the past and a thorough overhauling of the social system through terror and violence. They condoned this violence because it would be coercion of the few by the many, of the exploiters by the exploited, of the ruling class by the people. They also implied that the period during which this dictatorship of the working class would prevail would be brief. Finally, whatever dictatorial or totalitarian features the dictatorship of the proletariat would

---

*Assuming that in fact secular religion tends to impose dictatorship on the people in its attempt to create an earthly paradise, we must be aware at the same time that heavenly religion, by postponing paradise to the hereafter, falls into the danger of being indifferent to human misery which could be alleviated by rational action.

entail, Marx and Engels regarded it as but the transition to the Good Society, and inevitable albeit regrettable means to a moral end.

We must ask ourselves on what facts or presuppositions Marx and Engels based this glowing optimism. Was it not in conflict with their ambivalent appraisal of civilization, that is, with their belief that the material progress of humanity had led to increasing dehumanization? To be sure, if alienation is a consequence of the division of labor, the class struggle, and the unequal distribution of the means of production, then it follows that alienation might be cured once private property and the class struggle have been abolished. If it is correct to trace the growth of oppressive institutions and deceptive ideologies to the special needs of class-torn societies, then surely it follows that tyranny, exploitation, and superstition are likely to wither away once the class struggle is a feature of the past. Even within the terms of Marxist ideas, however, it is by no means obvious why the revolution leading to such a classless society should ever occur, or why, if indeed the working class seizes power, it will know what to do with it to ensure that leap into the realm of freedom that Engels and Marx foresaw. On the contrary, if they were right in saying that people are dehumanized under capitalism and that the worker has been transformed into a commodity, a marketable piece of equipment, how could they impute to these same workers that rationality which would make the coming of socialism inevitable?

The answer is that, according to Marxist theory, the proletariat is so absolutely alienated that the mechanism by which the ruling classes have usually managed to divert the attention and stultify the minds of the exploited no longer functions. The workers under capitalism have been estranged so relentlessly from what sociologists today call primary organizations and loyalties that their consciousness can free itself from deceptive ideologies. Having been dehumanized, the workers become aware of their dehumanization and understand the social system that has produced them. When people become conscious of themselves as commodities, they will feel the urge to abolish the mode of production that makes them commodities. They will also have the power to do so.

Marx and Engels attributed to the working class not only full rationality (born out of unprecedented misery) but also a number of qualities that would enable them to be successful in their striving to abolish capitalism. For one, the proletariat in the period of mature capitalism would constitute the overwhelming majority of the population. Moreover, they would be well organized, having learned the virtues of cooperation in the capitalist machine shop, where work proceeded in cooperative fashion. By drafting them into their armies, the ruling classes had also trained the proletariat for warfare, and by educating them in at least an elementary way had further equipped them for the coming role as revolutionaries and rulers. Finally, Marx and Engels assumed that as the class that by its physical labor with modern machines was the only really productive class in capitalist society, the proletariat was also well prepared to expropriate the means of production and assume command over them.

This image of the working class as combining rationality with power and therefore inevitably bound to lead humanity into the Promised Land is a bold attempt to reconcile the gloomy theory of alienation with the Promethean image. It must be regarded as the cornerstone of Marxist theory.

We recognize in this image a variation of a dream that is at least as old as Socrates. He believed that true goodness cannot be theoretical but must be expressed in works: One cannot know virtue without practicing it. Something akin to this belief is inherent in the Marxist belief that the self-consciousness of the proletariat will impel it to act. But Marx also shared the idea of Socrates' pupil Plato that ideas remain ineffectual if they are not backed by power. This insight into the problem of power caused Plato to wish for a philosopher who was either himself a king or whose advice was accepted by a king. In Marx the awareness of the problem of power led to the statement that ideas become effective only when they get hold of the masses. Neither philosophy nor action is effective by itself; they must work together. It is not enough, wrote Marx, that the idea strive toward realization; reality should also be receptive to the idea. And it is this coincidence of revolutionary thought with revolutionary action that Marx saw in the working-class movement on the eve of the revolution of 1848.

The reader might miss a treatment of Marxist philosophy in this short sketch, especially since almost any other treatment of Marxism, be it by communists or by Western scholars, would begin with an outline of dialectical materialism. The reason I am omitting such an outline is that Marxism is a social theory, not a universal philosophy. Marx was interested in human relationships and social institutions. He dealt with nature only insofar as it was part of human society, and he had use for philosophy only to the extent that it was identical with scientific method. He held, moreover, that every realm of existence must be understood in terms of its own laws; hence he did not contend that the methods and insights he advanced in his social theories were applicable to biology, physics, or general philosophy. There is, in short, a decidedly positivistic strain in Marxism. And yet, neither Marx nor Engels could escape or deny the profound influence that Hegelian philosophy exerted on them, a philosophy that focused its sights on concepts of reason and freedom and had developed a highly esoteric combination of ontology and logic, called dialectics. In negating these elements of Hegelian philosophy, Marx nonetheless retained and transformed it.

The Marxian dialectic is based on a recognition that reality, particularly the reality of all human relations, is beset by the perpetual tension between actuality and potentialities, between what is, what could be, and what ought to be. Because Engels and Marx were highly sensitive to this contradiction, their language is deliberately ambiguous, and their judgments are correspondingly ambivalent. All reality is seen within the context of historic development; past and present, present and future are seen as contained within each other, so that in this case, too, it is no longer possible to make simple, straightforward statements. Finally, the task of grasping the world is regarded as one in which intellectual comprehension must go hand in hand with the creative and destructive activity of remaking the world: Theory and practice merge into one.

Philosophy and politics, thought and action, science and moral postulates must coalesce, as Plato had hoped they would fuse in the philosopher-king. And just as the Platonic utopia demands a philosopher-king, so the entire structure of Marxist ideas is held together by the belief that the proletariat does indeed represent the merger of theory and practice. This belief, in turn, is the keystone of that "materialist" (read: sociological) dialectics into which Marx transformed Hegel's philosophy of reason. However, moral philosophy that becomes incarnate in the

CHAPTER 3

European Marxism

When Marx and Engels wrote the *Manifesto of the Communist party* in 1847, summarizing their views with marvelous conciseness, they seem to have been momentarily expecting the end of capitalism. They thought that their ideas were but the articulation of actual feelings, of the actual consciousness shared by vast masses of proletarians who were prepared for revolutionary action and were waiting only for some historic event or for action by the enlightened leadership to set events in motion. Marx and Engels knew, as many other politically conscious people in Europe knew, that a revolution was brewing. They thought it would be the revolution of the proletariat.*

In fact, however, the working class played a comparatively negligible role in most of the upheavals that shook Europe in 1848. Moreover, in the subsequent years and even decades, the development of the working-class movement gave Marx and Engels little encouragement to expect the proletariat to rally to the banner of their ideas. Working-class parties were slow in getting organized, and when they did, their leaders (and followers) were not necessarily committed to Marxist doctrines.

This failure of the 1848 revolution and the seeming unwillingness of the masses to become fully conscious (in the Marxist sense of the term) led to soul searching on the part of the fathers of the doctrine and caused them to make adjustments in their thoughts concerning the nature of capitalism, the aims and morphology of

---

*This idea is expressed clearly in *The Communist Manifesto;* in Marx's *The Poverty of Philosophy;* and in the essay by Engels on the *History of the Communist League.*

the revolution, and the strategy to be employed by the proletariat. Explanations had to be found for the failure; contemporary political constellations had to be examined for this purpose; and, in both cases, Engels and Marx were forced to pay closer attention to concrete phenomena at odds with the more abstract grand design of their theoretical model. Recognition of precapitalist features still affecting current politics was not, of course, regarded as a refutation of the theory, but it did complicate the task of analysis, self-orientation, and evaluation. Similarly, instead of preparing for the final act of revolution, as Engels, particularly, had done with joyous alacrity in 1848, Marx and Engels now felt compelled to study and discuss strategies that might prepare the ground for revolution and lead toward it. Here again short-range plans were likely to come into conflict with long-range expectations. Or, at least, the strategy of Marxist politics was obliged to consider measures and attitudes that the original theory of revolution simply had not incorporated—alliances with other radical movements, foreign policy problems, the evaluation of constitutional democracy from the point of view of the proletariat, and so forth. Various ranges of strategy were developed, and different aims—minimal, maximal, and in between—were formulated. In retrospect, many of these changes appear drastic when compared to the dreams of 1848, and one scholar has dramatized the contrast by stating that after 1848 Marx "became what is nowadays called an ex-Communist."*

Yet these drastic changes did not imply any fundamental changes in the grand conception. Rather, they can be regarded as refinements, concretization, elaboration, and extension of the doctrine. The intense and ceaseless intellectual activity of research, writing, and debating in which Marx and Engels engaged to the end of their lives, without ever completing their major task of systematic exposition, was solidly founded on the ideas they had elaborated in common in the five years or so before 1848.

This unfinished job of elaboration and extension made Marxism more complex, ambiguous, and fragmentary, hence more subject to controversial discussion, misinterpretation, and vulgarization. There are, indeed, many scholars who claim that the

* George Lichtheim, "Marxist Doctrine in Perspective," *Problems of Communism*, VII, No. 6 (March-April 1958), p. 34.

process of misinterpretation and vulgarization was begun by Engels himself. They argue that Engels's book against Dühring, his unpublished essays on the history of science, and many other pronouncements are filled with naive and shallow passages that do violence to Marx's sophistication, and that his attempt to apply Marxist ideas to the realm of natural science is based on misunderstanding. However, Marx approved the anti-Dühring manuscript and had parts of it translated. Moreover, most of the alleged misinterpretations can be supported by statements Marx himself made. We must realize that the ideas of Marx were not of one piece; they have remained fragmentary, obscure, and contradictory. Both Engels and Marx grew and learned and changed, shifting their attention from one problem to another and changing their views as well. Much of their work remained unpublished until well after their deaths. As a result, they were not always well understood even by people who thought themselves their followers, and observing this, Marx himself often felt inclined to dissociate himself from those who purported to speak in his name.

Indeed, Engels and Marx did not have much of a following of any kind until late in their lives. Marx died in 1883 and Engels died in 1895. It was only in the 1870s that Marx became well known and his name associated with a large working-class movement. That movement then developed rapidly, especially in Germany, where industrialization had begun late and was going on at a feverish pace, developing large concentrations of workers in quickly growing cities.

With its authoritarian culture and its sharp class divisions, Germany was ripe for the kind of revolutionary proletarian movement Marx and Engels had foreseen and desired. German Marxism grew to a party that attracted millions of voters and hundreds of thousands of members, and it sent increasing numbers of deputies into the German parliament, the *Reichstag*. The government outlawed it in 1878 but did not manage to destroy it. Instead, twelve years of persecution and illegality embittered and ultimately strengthened the movement, so that in 1890 it reemerged with a strong organization and an equally strong will to come to power. In its structure, its ideas, and its functioning, it had adapted itself well to its environment and, in turn, imparted much of the spirit of that environment to European Marxism in general.

I would suggest that Marxism between 1890 and 1914 should be regarded as a *"Prussianization"* of the movement. It was Prussian in the way it combined tough talk with cautious action; Prussian in its insistence on centralized organization, command-like leadership, bureaucratic management, and unquestioning discipline; Prussian also in the uncomradely tone that its members adopted in political discussion. At the same time Marxism in the 1890s took on much of the general Victorian culture then prevalent throughout Europe: It managed to blend the ideas of Marx and Engels with those of Darwin and with the late nineteenth-century worship of natural science. It spoke in tones dripping with moral indignation even while stoutly denying the validity of moral arguments. It reduced all politics, all culture, all social phenomena to economic terms and evaluated all human endeavors in narrow utilitarian fashion—did they or did they not promote the victory of the proletariat? It was stuffy in its attitude on manners, mores, and culture, frowning on avant-gardist experiments in artistic, sexual, and related concerns. All these trends implied subtle but deep changes in the nature of Marxist ideology, and many scholars would argue that most of these changes amounted to an impoverishment.

An impoverishment of thought also took place because the leaders of the movement, in their attempt to make Marxism palatable to the masses, transformed a subtle, sophisticated philosophy into simple slogans that were often little more than invective—shouts of indignation or encouragement. Moreover, a growing discrepancy appeared between theory and practice. In theory and rhetoric the movement was uncompromising and revolutionary. So also was some of its practice: The Marxist leadership allowed no collaboration with parties or individuals outside the movement. It preached a doctrine of exclusivism. The only aim of election campaigns and party politics that it recognized was that of preparing for victory. This victory was firmly expected and taken for granted, and in retrospect, it is clear that the European Marxist movement did little to bring it about. Its militant rhetoric masked a politics of passivity or at least of caution. There were several reasons for this: First, the period of underground struggle in Germany, 1878–1890, had not been comfortable by any means. While it had made the party leadership bitter, it also made them eager not to provoke the authorities once again. Even more important, the working class at the turn of the century was different from that described by Engels around 1840. Far from being impoverished, it was beginning to obtain its share—however modest—of the material benefits being reaped by the business community in these decades. Moreover, whether because of the continued agitation for constitutional reform, or for whatever other reasons, the working class was given the franchise, formed political parties, and began to participate in constitutional politics.

Instead of being absolutely alienated, therefore, significant sections of the working class, and especially their political leaders and trade-union officials, began to feel themselves part of a functioning social system that only needed to be improved to be altogether acceptable. From revolutionists they turned into reformists and constitutional democrats. Abandoning the plan to smash the existing system, they began to strive for improvements in working and living conditions and for equal political rights. And in the end, when an international war forced them to decide between their loyalty to their class and their loyalty to their country, most of them, at least for the time being, abandoned internationalism and chose patriotism.

There was therefore a growing gap between the revolutionary theory and the reformist practice of the Marxist movement, which sooner or later would call for serious readjustments. Most of those who were aware of the discrepancy sought to revise Marxist ideas to bring them into line with current political strategies. Their efforts aroused fierce resistance from those for whom Marxism had become a set of dogmas totally beyond challenge. They denounced all suggestions that times had changed and that Marxism therefore deserved to be reexamined, as *revisionism*.

What was then called revisionism consisted of several kinds of challenge to orthodoxy. I would single out two different but overlapping lines of criticism. First, there were the attempts to bring the theory and rhetoric of the movement in line with its reformist, antirevolutionary practice, to redefine the goals and the tactics of the movement, as well as its analysis of capitalism, accordingly. Capitalism was recognized as working better and having greater staying power than Engels and Marx had assumed. The goal of the movement, according to such revisionists as Eduard Bernstein, should be gradual reform of capitalism, not its abolition, and in their struggle for reform, the workers' movement should ally itself with progressive forces outside the party. All forces to the left of center ought to unite at least for the purpose of defeating the reactionary establishment. One might refer to this kind of revisionism as the liberalization of Marxism. It has been a persistent trend in the European working-class parties ever since the 1890s.

A very different aim was pursued by other Marxist leaders who often were lumped together with the liberalizers. These were people in the movement who deplored the narrowness of its aims, the exclusive attention paid to economic concerns, and the class struggle. They argued, in effect, that alienation and oppression take many forms and that a movement fighting to liberate humanity from oppression ought to pay attention to all these evils and fight against them as determinedly as it was fighting against wage slavery. Thus they proposed that the Marxist movement fight against the oppression of women and the miseducation of the young, against the despoliation of nature and the repression of sexuality. They proposed that it recognize the power of avant-gardist art and literature in raising people's consciousness and that it resist the aesthetic impoverishment caused by mass culture and kitsch. In short, revisionists of this kind demanded that the movement ally itself with the most radical wings of the women's movement, the intellectual avant garde, movements for sexual liberation, and the like. In effect, this branch of revisionism can be seen as an attempt not to liberalize Marxism but to radicalize it by broadening its scope and making it break out of the shell of Victorian culture. This trend, too, has recurred many times in the history of Marxism.

CHAPTER 4

Leninism

The success of Marxism in becoming the dominant ideology of the European working-class movement would eventually make it attractive to radical intellectuals throughout the world. Just as German Marxism around the turn of the century reflected prevalent Victorian views and Prussian political culture, so once Marxist doctrines were brought to Russia, the ideas and the practices of the movement underwent a process of Russification. I would, in fact, define Leninism as Russified Marxism.

The tsarist empire must be characterized as a relatively "backward" society, a term that is not meant to imply moral or cultural superiority of other nations but to denote only one thing, technological inferiority and the resultant lower productivity. Nor does it imply that the country did not have its share of highly educated, cultured people who made important contributions to science, art, and philosophy. Russia before the revolution of 1917 was backward because in the nations of Western and Central Europe she faced neighbors who had more productive economies and therefore were also stronger militarily and politically. In stressing the nicely measurable economic backwardness, I do not, of course, wish to minimize related cultural and political differences, such as the almost universal illiteracy of the Russian people through the nineteenth century or the prevalence of an autocratic political system of the kind that the French and American revolutions had done away with more than a hundred years before.

Economically advanced nations are usually regarded by their less-fortunate neighbors as presenting a threat to themselves, and much of Russia's history can be explained in terms of reaction to the technological superiority of the West. The great dilemma faced by political leaders in underdeveloped areas is this: What they regard as the threat of economically advanced nations can be mitigated only by adopting the technology which is at the basis of the presumed threat. For a nation that wishes to maintain its established culture and traditional way of life, the need to "westernize" is extremely painful. But the rulers of old Russia were well aware of this need, and some of Russia's tsars were nothing less than revolutionaries who tried to transform radically the society over which they ruled. To be sure, while they sought to introduce Western technology, science, and administrative skills, they did not wish to endanger their own rule. Consequently, their aim was to westernize selectively, but in this they did not succeed. On the contrary, with Western technology and administration came Western progressive ideas and movements of reform.

Old Russia was ruled by emperors who claimed absolute power. Their arm of government was a civil and military bureaucracy, the officers of which were recruited mainly from the landowning aristocracy, a privileged leisure class whose wealth was measured not only in land but also in serfs. They had obtained their privileges as compensation for services rendered to the tsars. But in the eighteenth century they were freed of their service obligation while retaining their privileges. Indeed, service itself became a privilege of the nobility. After the nobles were freed of their duties, the serfs remained in bondage for about another hundred years. They were released only in the second half of the nineteenth century. But the land they were given at this time was so inadequate that they remained in economic bondage to their old masters. Constantly on the brink of economic ruin and smarting under legal discrimination, the Russian peasants, constituting about nine-tenths of the population, were therefore a dissatisfied class and potential fomenters of revolution.

Toward the end of the nineteenth century, industry began to develop in Russia and a working class grew. The working class found itself laboring and living under very poor conditions, thus forming another revolutionary class, which was easy to organize and from the very beginning was conscious of its grievances. With the growth of industrialism, a middle class of merchants, capitalists, and well-educated professional people also arose. This class at once sought to participate in the political process and began to advance such aims as free enterprise and democracy. In tsarist Russia such aims, too, were revolutionary. These political- ly dissatisfied groups were joined by representatives of Russia's numerous national minorities, who demanded equality, auton- omy, self-determination, and similar rights which tsarist Russia denied them. These classes were potentially revolutionary in the sense that their grievances were deep and the system was unable or too dilatory to satisfy them. My calling them revolutionary does not, however, mean that Russia's peasants, workers, and growing middle class were active in fomenting revolution or even desirous of overthrowing tsarism. On the contrary, the vast majority of Rus- sians doubtless felt that their needs and hopes could and would be satisfied by the tsar and his government. Only dramatic crises of confidence jolted sufficient numbers out of this belief to cause revolutionary upheavals.

Russia had witnessed rebellion, unrest, and revolution through- out the ages. But the revolutions of 1905 and 1917 were unique because in them for the first time the entire people, or at least the vast majority, participated actively or tolerated the upheaval passively. These revolutions were different also because, unlike most previous rebellions Russia had witnessed, they were fought in the name of ideals imported from the West: the ideals of liberalism and socialism. Finally, in 1917, these ideals were being propounded and translated into programs and strategies by organized political parties well known to the broad masses of the population.

Nineteenth-century Russia had proved to be curiously recep- tive to the most radical Western ideas, and beginning in the 1880s, Marxism began to exert tremendous influence on the minds of revolutionary intellectuals. Out of local conspiratorial organizations, which often began to coalesce with the spontan- eously growing labor movement, a Marxist party was born, and by 1903 it emerged fully organized, though troubled by serious disagreements. In fact, we can easily agree with Leopold Haim- son, who says that the Russian Social-Democratic Labor party in 1903 was stillborn: The disagreements dividing the party in the very beginning of its history became more and more acute. Fac- tions developed into separate parties, and the contending leaders finally found themselves on opposite sides of the barricades.

These disagreements can be traced to the difficulties that inevitably arose when attempts were made to apply Marxist ideas to Russia. It should be obvious that the thoughts of Marx and Engels about the nature of the revolution or about political strategy could not serve as an adequate guide to their Russian disciples. Marxism was the product of Western conditions and Western developments, and many features of Russian society did not correspond to the Marxist model. Marx and Engels had relied on a large and mature proletariat to seize power when the number of capitalists had been reduced to a minimum. In Russia, however, the number of workers was small in comparison with the total population. Moreover, capitalism, far from being on the decline or even at its peak, was still growing. The number of people engaged in business was small—not, however, because competition had ruined most of them, but rather because Russian capitalism was still in its beginnings. Russia remained overwhelmingly a country of peasants. Who was to serve as the historical moving force in such a country? Who was to play the revolutionary role most Marxists wanted to be played?

And what kind of revolution was it to be? It could not very well be expected that a proletarian revolution in Russia—or any revolution whatsoever—would usher in the socialist society predicted by Marx and Engels. Russia's peasant society could not produce that abundance of industrial products which, in Marxist theory, is one of the essential preconditions of socialism. Hence even a proletarian revolution in Russia would have to have different results from those expected in the West.

Every one of these and related questions raised controversies that created and exacerbated division in the Russian Marxist movement. Obviously, it would not be possible within the framework of this study to trace any of these controversies. Since our topic is communism, we must, in any event, largely disregard the arguments of noncommunist Marxists. Hence we will not discuss the views of the Mensheviks at all. But even the Bolsheviks' views can be summarized only in the sketchiest manner.*

Bolsheviks and Mensheviks agreed that in Russia the working

---

*For a more detailed presentation of my views, and for sources, see Alfred G. Meyer, *Leninism* (Cambridge, Mass., 1957), of which the present chapter is a brief abstract.

class must fight for not one but two revolutions—the bourgeois and the proletarian one. Their political program thus gave unprecedentedly sharp emphasis to the Marxist distinction between maximal and minimal goals. The Bolsheviks' minimum program aimed to destroy tsarism and the rule of landlords and to establish a "democratic republic," that is, a constitutional, representative government, in which, to be sure, social legislation providing for social security, minimum wages, maximum hours, and the like, was to protect the working class against excessive exploitation. Only after this stage had been reached would it be advisable to begin preparations for the proletarian revolution that would usher in the socialist society.

This step-by-step approach to socialism was dictated by the developmental theory of Marxism, which sees history as a logical unfolding of stages where the contradictions or inconsistencies inherent in each stage determine the nature of the succeeding one. Few Marxists even in Russia were prepared to admit the possibility that any major stage might be skipped altogether, though in practice Bolshevik theory was to come close to this position, as we shall see.

The Bolshevik's endeavor to help establish a "democratic republic" in Russia can be explained by another argument as well: Communism was convinced (and communists today tend to have similar convictions) that constitutional democracy was more desirable than the tsarist police state or any other autocratic government.

The Bolshevik attitude toward democracy is highly complex. In the sense of popular government, democracy is, of course, part of the ideal toward which Marxism and Leninism are striving. The idea of the withering away of government in favor of some sort of anarchic communalism is but the most radical formulation of democratic ideals, as Marx himself was eager to point out. It was to be accomplished by abolishing the rule of special interests (ruling classes), which alone, in the eyes of Marx, made the existence of repressive governmental institutions necessary. Once classes were abolished, repressive institutions would become unnecessary and would gradually disappear. In Marxist theory the fulfillment of the liberal ideal is thus seen as a by-product of the fulfillment of socialist ideals. All these notions linger on in the political ideals by which communist parties and communist regimes justify their existence, even though few if any adherents pretend these days that they are close to being achieved.

But there has been controversy within the Bolshevik's camp over the question whether the classless society, and the democracy that goes with it, can be attained through democratic processes of representative, constitutional government. On the one hand, Marxism is based on the belief that the working class is rational. A consequence of this belief is a general faith in democratic processes, and for this reason Marxist politicians have generally been in favor of constitutional government, widening of the franchise, civil liberties, and the like. These rights and advantages might have to be won by a revolution (which would, of course, be the bourgeois revolution). But, once won, they would assure the victory of the proletariat. Or rather, once constitutional democracy was fully realized, the proletariat, constituting the vast majority of the people, would be in power. Engels could therefore say that the democratic republic would be the specific form of the dictatorship of the proletariat.

The Russian communists, however, could not follow Marx and Engels all the way in these thoughts. For in Russia, where the proletariat was still in the minority, the democratic republic would not spell proletarian rule. Yet, untrammeled democracy could nonetheless be very useful to the proletarian movement as a stepping stone toward the proletarian dictatorship, and for this reason it was the main plank of the minimum platform. We can best understand this if we realize that Russian revolutionary intellectuals instinctively contrasted the word *democracy* with autocracy and bureaucracy. To them, it therefore signified not so much constitutional government or any government whatsoever, but rather the absence of restraint and direct rule by the masses. Like Marx, they interpreted the concept of democracy in the spirit of Rousseau, that is, as that direct rule of the people of which Hamilton, Madison, and most of the other American Founding Fathers were so keenly afraid. According to Marxist theory, however, the absence of governmental restraints in capitalist society could mean only open class warfare, for the absense of such restraints would cause all the contradictions of capitalism to come to the surface and clearly divide society. Democracy therefore becomes synonymous with civil war. Such a clear and open struggle, however, would be desirable because it could end only with the victory of the proletariat.

To be sure, Bolshevik strategy also took into account the fact that democratic government can be equated with constitutional, representative government, which customarily provides political liberties for all citizens, and the establishment of such a government in place of more authoritarian forms is desirable because the communist movement, like all interest groups, would like to operate as freely as possible. Moreover, the mere struggle for political liberties would benefit the communist movement whether it was successful or not. Success would give desired advantages. Failure could be used for the purpose of buttressing the communists' argument that under capitalism democracy will always be imperfect.

Hence Bolsheviks fight with unrelenting vigor to establish and perfect constitutional democracy. Win or lose, the fight will pay off. And yet, we can detect a certain hesitancy about this, a certain preference for losing the fight. For communism has remained highly suspicious of the liberties granted under constitutional government. While democratic institutions might be regarded as an aid in revolutionary struggle, communists of the Leninist persuasion warn that a Marxist should never fall victim to "constitutional illusions," that is, to the belief that capitalism can be overthrown and socialism established without violence and revolution. Bourgeois democracy, wrote Lenin, "is always narrow, hypocritical, mendacious, and false; it always remains democracy for the rich, a bluff for the poor."* While he criticized those of his comrades who did not recognize the advantages of utilizing the freedoms of representative government, he was even more critical of those who thought that the fight for democratic liberties was an end in itself. Such an overemphasis of the minimum program, he thought, amounted to a betrayal of the proletarian revolution. Bolshevik communism thus has a highly ambivalent attitude toward piecemeal gains: They are useful and must be used, but they also threaten to corrupt those who gain advantages from them.

The precise relationship of their minimum goal to the final and overall aims of the movement was not the only problem troubling the Russian communists. Circumstances also caused them at various times to redefine the minimum goal itself: Although in their purist moods communist theoreticians have asserted that

* V. I. Lenin, *Sochineniia* [Works] 2d ed., XXIII (Moscow, 1931), p. 220.

there is no essential difference between various types of capitalist society, practical politics impelled them at other times to voice a preference for one or another such type as the minimal goal to strive for. Furthermore, it has always been a thorny problem for them to decide precisely what forces in underdeveloped societies such as Russia were to carry out this bourgeois revolution. Russian communists were agreed that in their country the *bourgeois revolution* would have to be carried out or at least initiated and led *by the proletariat*—a curious but extremely important variation on the original Marxist theme. But, obviously, a proletariat constituting a small minority could not by itself carry out this revolution. Who should be its allies? And how should such allies be attracted to the party of the proletariat? In answering these questions communism has played it by ear, but after a good deal of controversy, the Russian pattern of 1917 has emerged as the school solution: According to this pattern, the proletariat is to carry out the bourgeois revolution aided by the land-hungry peasantry, by dissatisfied national or other minorities, and possibly even by sections of the liberal middle class wherever this class can be expected to be ready for revolutionary action. In colonial countries, virtually every class might be deemed a suitable ally. The proletariat is to attract these auxiliary forces by adopting their specific grievances and aspirations as planks in its own political platform and is to promote these aspirations in the most vigorous and radical fashion, so as to steal all other revolutionary parties' thunder. Communist programs in underdeveloped countries therefore typically include demands for radical land reform and for national self-determination.

While stressing the need for alliances and for the theoretical and political flexibility that would make such alliances possible, communist doctrine stresses even more the idea that in all such political arrangements the proletariat must retain a leading role. Proletarian hegemony in the bourgeois revolution, paradoxical as it may sound, is demanded by communist strategy for several reasons. For one thing, Lenin was convinced that, in Russia at least, the bourgeoisie was not interested enough in ''its own'' revolution to promote it without being pushed by the working class, or as a variant of this, he tended to believe that precisely because of vigorous proletarian initiative the bourgeoisie was not interested. In any event, he assumed that the bourgeoisie could not be expected to promote the bourgeois revolution. And, once the revolution had begun, the bourgeoisie could be expected to work against it or to betray it by making compromises with the old ruling class. Finally, he argued that proletarian hegemony in the bourgeois revolution would ease the transition to the next stage—the proletarian revolution.

We are touching here yet another problem concerning the relationship between the two revolutions: How can the party make sure that the transition from the bourgeois to a socialist society is effected most swiftly and efficiently? For, after all, as soon as it has been reached, the minimum goal turns into an obstacle, into something hostile that must be overcome, or at best, it is regarded as a stepping stone toward the higher goal. In no case, however, is it something desirable in its own right. On the contrary, the longer the phase between the bourgeois revolution and the proletarian revolution lasts, the more time given the bourgeois regime to entrench itself, the more difficult will it be to complete the series of revolutions. Communist theory has remained ambiguous about this problem. Estimates of the desirable or probable time span that would separate one from the other have ranged from Vladimir Lenin's "era of world wars and revolutions" to Leon Trotsky's hope that the two revolutions might merge and occur simultaneously, an idea that was based on thoughts vaguely expressed by Marx and Engels in the *Communist Manifesto*. (Even the Trotskyist term "permanent revolution" was used by Marx and Engels in this context.) In between we have another idea of Lenin's, namely, that the democratic republic established by the proletariat in the bourgeois revolution would slowly but surely "grow over" into socialism.

The Marxist-Leninist program for Russia was further refined and complicated by linking it with the expected world revolution—partly in order to better justify revolutionary action by the Marxist movement in a backward country. Many of the daring schemes constituting the Russian communist program were so bold a departure from the original Marxist scheme that many other Marxist theoreticians looked upon Lenin's party as a group of unprincipled adventurers lusting for power regardless of the consequences. They argued that Russia was in no wise prepared (or "mature") for a proletarian regime, and that therefore a Russian revolution carried out under proletarian hegemony could not but lead to failure and would discredit the entire Marxist movement.

Bolsheviks agreed that a proletarian revolution in Russia alone made no sense. Yet when the chance came to seize power, they seized it in the name of the proletariat. But whether or not they were in fact unprincipled adventurers, they did have a theoretical justification for their action. I have called the arguments they used the theory of the spark. Just as Lenin insisted that the working class as the most conscious element of society would set the bourgeois revolution in motion by its own initiative, so he asserted that the proletarian revolution in Russia (doomed to failure if it were an isolated event) would spark a world-wide chain reaction of proletarian revolution. This world revolution, in turn, would ensure the success of socialism even in such a backward country as Russia. Here we see that even in Lenin's view the bourgeois and the proletarian revolutions have merged into one event.

THE PARTY

Marx and Engels were concerned primarily with prognoses, that is, trends of development they thought they recognized in present-day reality; this preoccupation resulted from necessity, not choice. Lenin, however, stressed plans and wishes, goals and desiderata. Marx and Engels were confident that reality would develop toward the goal. Lenin knew what the goal was and made the most determined efforts to reach it. To be sure, they all asserted the inevitability of socialism. But I think that we can detect a subtle change in this notion of inevitability. For Engels and Marx it had been a concrete certainty of events to come in the immediate future. For Lenin it was far more theoretical than that. And theory in this case was always in danger of being divorced from practice. Theoretically socialism was inevitable; any convinced Marxist was sure of that. But practically it would take careful planning and adjustments to make it come about. Theory, in short, was no longer an expression of what was, that is, scientific analysis and description; instead, it had become a guide to action, a method of analyzing and understanding reality in such a fashion that it could be used for the attainment of the goals the theory had developed.

By emphasizing goals, communism prepared to discard the

means, procedures, and patterns of development that Marx and Engels had foreseen or described. The validity of their scheme of evolution was never challenged directly, but in the hands of communist political leaders it became more and more schematic and abstract. At the same time, communist theory gave even greater emphasis than Marx and Engels had given to theory itself as a creative force in history.

Communism as developed by Lenin is a school of Marxism that assigns a tremendously important role to rational understanding, which they call *consciousness*. To communists it is the most essential force in history. For, without scientific knowledge, or rather, without leadership by people possessing such knowledge, chaos and disaster instead of socialism might be the outcome of history.

Communism complements its demand for proletarian hegemony with the equally insistent striving for the hegemony of consciousness. Hegemony over what? Over insufficiently developed consciousness, that is, over instinct, habit, tradition—in short, over any political action which is not based on the scientific (read: Marxist) understanding of reality. Communist theory defines nonconscious political action as *spontaneous*, and the hegemony of consciousness is therefore to be established over spontaneity.

Conceptually, this is not different from the Marxist theory, in which the proletariat was assigned its Chosen People role precisely because consciousness was attributed to it. Because Marx did attribute consciousness to the working class, however, he had no need to differentiate theoretically between consciousness and spontaneity. The *Communist Manifesto* refers to the party as an organization providing theoretical and practical leadership and mentions bourgeois intellectuals who, by virtue of their enlightment and insight, break away from their own class and provide this leadership for the proletariat. But the implication remains nonetheless that the spontaneous emergence of class consciousness in the proletariat itself is inevitable. Consciousness and spontaneity coincide in the theory of Engels and Marx.

In Leninist theory they do not. On the contrary, by itself (that means spontaneously) the working class would never attain consciousness. Consequently, it would never be able to carry out its historic task, or at least not alone.

Nonetheless, consciousness must guide the proletariat. And if the working class by itself cannot attain it, it must be found elsewhere. Lenin asserted that it was possessed by educated people, intellectuals such as he. It is they whom consciousness compels to prepare and lead the proletariat in the revolutions that have to be staged in Russia. They are expected to provide this leadership by devoting their entire lives to the task, becoming revolutionaries by profession. They are the ones who should form the party, which Lenin conceived as consciousness incarnate or institutionalized, the *Ecclesia Militans* of history, the general staff of the proletarian revolutions. And, because Leninism relies so firmly on consciousness for deliverance, it must rely with equal fervor on the strength and the survival of the party in which consciousness has become flesh. Come what may, the party must be preserved. Without it the proletariat is nothing. Without it everything is lost.

Leninism therefore incorporated a theory of leadership and thus reversed a tendency in the writings of Engels and Marx, who seem to have believed that any revolution that has leaders will fail. In their view, leaders mislead. They cannot liberate anyone from bondage or exploitation, because the only genuine liberation is self-liberation. All initiative in genuine socialist democracy must come from the masses of the people at the grass roots, and without democracy there cannot be socialism.

Lenin, in contrast, believed the masses to be incapable of self-emancipation. For him, democracy at least in its initial phases would be government for, but not by, the people. For him the revolution was analogous to a battle, and in battle the troops must be led by officers, who are guided by a general staff. For him, the party was this general staff.

A general staff by itself, however, cannot wage nor win a battle. A party formed only by the enlightened few is unable to win revolutions. To do so, the vanguard of the proletariat must be sure that the rank and file of the working class will act according to its commands. In addition, the party must aim to go beyond the working class in attracting the allies which, as we have seen, the proletariat in "backward" countries needs.

All political parties seek to gain adherents and become decisive majorities. In order to do so, parties customarily try to develop programs and voice slogans that respond to the felt or anticipated needs of potential political adherents. They try to voice the will of the people or of important groups within the people.

The Communist party cannot gain adherents quite so simply. Since it believes that it is the repository of consciousness, while the people, including even the proletariat, are incapable of defining their own interests, the party obviously cannot let the "spontaneous" feelings of the masses determine policy. On the contrary, its consciousness, and the goals and policies derived from it, must somehow be instilled in, or imposed on, the people whom the party wishes to lead. What is required, then, is an educational job, and indeed the party regards its most important function to be the education of the proletariat. The consciousness that the party possesses must be given to the working class.

Communist theorists refer to this educational work as *propaganda,* but they do not wish to imply by the use of this word irrational, tricky, or deceptive means of persuasion. On the contrary, propaganda denotes the painful and lengthy effort of so educating the proletariat that it understands and absorbs Marxist theory in all its ramifications and complications. For only this constitutes consciousness. There are, however, means short of this difficult process, which the party uses to gain adherents. There are, for instance, the important first steps of the educational effort, measures designed to wake up the masses and plant the first seeds of consciousness in their minds. These first steps are short and simple messages—slogans—dramatizing the workers' grievances and providing greatly simplified explanations for them. Collectively, these primitive efforts to arouse resentment against capitalism and faith in communism are called *agitation.* Its messages are no more meant to be deceptive than those of propaganda; they are only simplified truths which even simple minds can grasp.

Education to consciousness, however, is not enough. Communist theorists have great difficulty deciding how much effort and time is required to raise the workers' level of consciousness. Estimates have varied according to circumstances. In times of revolution or impending revolution, the party has tended to be optimistic about this problem. At other times, its leaders were aware of the difficulties they faced in educating the masses.

Yet the party needs the masses to carry out its policies. Moreover, communism is impatient Marxism, which cannot afford to wait for the proletariat to become mature, just as in Russia it could not wait until the society had finally caught up with Western Europe in its development. At least one Western scholar maintains that this "impatience" was inherent in the Marxist movement long before Lenin, and therefore Marxism, by the very mood it expresses and by the structure of its principal ideas, is suited primarily or only to countries in the very early stages of industrial and capitalist development.* In the communist (Bolshevik) branch of the Russian Marxist movement, this impatience is the result of suppressed but strong and persistent doubts concerning the inevitability of socialism, doubts that in their turn are related not only to the unpropitious Russian environment but also to those changes in the nature of the working-class movement that led to the changes in Western Marxist doctrines (see Chapter 3). More generally yet, these doubts are a product of that era of "imperialism" which, as we will see, communist theory analyzes as the current stage of capitalist development. All these doubts have, as I phrased it above, made the idea of the inevitability of socialism more "theoretical."

Under the impact of the transformation of capitalism into imperialism and of the working class into an antirevolutionary interest group, most Marxist theorists in the West around 1900 abandoned revolutionary change. The Leninist solution of the same problem was different. Unwilling and, under Russian conditions, probably unable to abandon revolution as the means to attain socialism, communism found itself compelled to supplement the time-consuming method of education with more immediately effective manipulation of the masses. The party formulates goals and strategies. All that the masses have to do is to act according to the party's directives. To the communist it does not really matter whether or not the masses understand what they are doing. It may be desirable and preferable, but it is not essential.

Communism attributes consciousness to an elite of professional revolutionaries organized in the party. This party almost desperately feels the urge to act, so as to make its theory come true. Hence the masses, and in particular the proletariat, which in Marxist theory was the main agent of historic change, now turn into the main tools of such change. They become instruments in the hands of the conscious vanguard, raw material of revolutionary history, which must be molded and shaped and sent into action according to the party's plans.

* See Adam Ulam, *The Unfinished Revolution* (New York, 1960).

The party's principal means for working with this human raw material is not, as many might suppose, the use of irrational or deceptive means of persuasion, even though in fact there is no firm line between honest conviction and calculated appeal in the propaganda and agitation messages of communism; moreover, many policies (apart from propaganda or education) are adopted by the party, not for their own sake, but only because they are apt to attract followers and sympathizers, or because not adopting them would disillusion those whose sympathies already are with the party. As a matter of fact, communism is often torn by a sharp dilemma: Should the party remain true to its convictions even though its orthodox stand will alienate its followers, or should it be flexible, opportunistic, obedient in some fashion to grass-roots opinion, in order to attract the masses? Unwilling to wait until the masses become conscious, the party has usually decided that some concessions to their opinions must be made. Propaganda, in the sense of manipulation, thus plays its role. But another method of manipulating the masses is far more important and desirable, because it requires no concessions to grass-roots spontaneity. That method is organization.

Lenin, in some ways rather old-fashioned, was nonetheless up-to-date in a number of ways. One trait that made him a pioneer of twentieth-century politics was his insight into the crucial role of organization. Lenin realized that in modern industrial society (if not everywhere else) each human being is never an isolated individual. All human activities, economic, political, recreational, educational, and so forth, are carried out in and through organizations and associations. All individuals are functioning members of society only as members of the various groups to which they belong. And much of their behavior is influenced by these groups. Lenin concluded from this that masses of people could be influenced and manipulated most effectively if the manipulators were in control of the organizations and associations to which these masses belonged. Once the party controlled them, these organizations would become transmission belts (to use Lenin's phrase) conveying the will and impetus of the party leaders to the masses. Organization would be a system of wires the party could pull to set the people dancing to its tune. In this relationship, the lack of consciousness on the part of the masses did not really matter.

The Leninist party is therefore far more than a small elite of professional revolutionaries organized as leaders because they consider themselves conscious. It is also an educational institution aiming to raise the working class to the level of consciousness, and finally, it is the center of a vast network of auxiliary organizations, reaching—ideally—into every part of society in an attempt to control the entire associational life of broad masses of the population. The party's ideal is, of course, to dominate all of society in this indirect fashion. Needless to say, this dream comes close to being realized only after the party has come to power. Then, however, it becomes one of the guiding principles of communist government.*

DECISION-MAKING PROCESSES

The manipulative attitude with which we have become acquainted here is at the basis of the party's ideas on organization, and it pervades and shapes the party's political strategy. The party views not only the working classes as political raw material that should be organized and controlled; it similarly views all forces, arrangements, institutions—in short, everything that exists in contemporary society. In principle, the communist is ready and eager to regard everything as a potential instrument which, if wielded correctly and kept under control, can serve the party's and the movement's interests. Here we see a tendency toward the dissolution of the Marxist scheme of action into Machiavellian opportunism and amoral ruthlessness. And yet, this flexibility of strategy, this readiness to adjust action to the given environment, is neither unprincipled nor un-Marxist. Whatever the communist may do, he or she feels guided by principles insofar as he or she wants to work for the proletarian revolution and for socialism. Meanwhile, whatever the strategies, the communist can remain a Marxist as long as he or she keeps analyzing the environment in Marxist terms. Whatever he or she does, Marxism remains a guide to action as long as it guides his or her thinking.†

*See Chapter 7.

†Other writers disagree with this, having reduced communism to purely Machiavellian principles of expediency or to a code of behavior derived from irrational attitudes closely akin to paranoia (see Nathan Leites, *A Study of Bolshevism*, Chicago, 1953). These writers see communism as pursuing only one aim—power unlimited in scope and area. In their view, communism is absolutely unprincipled and immoral, the ideology serving only as rationalization of the urge to dominate. Most popular and journalistic books on the subject take this line, which I believe is based on inadequate understanding of the nature and history of Bolshevism. Once this view is accepted, the study of the development of communist ideas becomes, of course, quite irrelevant.

Communist theorists would strongly repudiate the inference that their movement is immoral or even amoral; on the contrary, they would stress the moral probity of communism and would claim that communist morality is the only valid morality of the contemporary world. They would point out that communism is based on, and in a broad sense guided by, moral indignation over capitalist inhumanity and by moral ideals concerning a society worthy of humanity, and communists are ever ready to measure others by their moral yardstick. The communist movement, moreover, is eager and impatient to make its ideal into reality. It wants action and success. Success in an evil world, however, is attainable only by working within that world and using the means that are at the movement's disposal. The *practical* morality of the communist movement is therefore a morality of expediency: Whatever works is moral; whatever does not is immoral. Whoever because of moral scruples fails to act resolutely to bring socialism nearer is a traitor to the morally just cause of communism. Whoever overcomes his or her "petty-bourgeois" moral scruples, whoever is unafraid to dirty his or her hands in the noble work of removing obstacles in the path of moral progress, is worthy of praise. Communism thus adopts the old maxim first attributed to the Jesuits, that the end justifies the means. A Westerner's first instinct is to point out that this contradicts prevalent Western notions of morality.* But I am not convinced that this is so. After all, we too argue that for the defense of certain ethical values we must be prepared to kill. We are ready to scrap conventional morals for causes we consider to be just. I suspect, therefore, that the main disagreement between the communists and their antagonists is over the ends, not over the means. Perhaps the communists are just more defiant and frank in stating the problem clearly and facing up to a morality of expediency.

At the same time, the manipulative attitude makes it more and more difficult to make decisions and to determine precisely what the proper Marxist course would be. The reason for this is that the manipulative attitude is linked with a profound ambivalence toward everything that exists. Everything—classes, groups, nations, institutions, attitudes, traditions—is potentially useful

---

*For books on communism which emphasize this Machiavellian morality of expediency, see Philip Selznick, *The Organizationl Weapon* (New York, 1952), and Stefan T. Possony, *A Century of Conflict* (Chicago, 1953).

to the party. But everything is at the same time part of the hated present. Everything is both an obstacle and a stepping stone on the road to progress. And Marxist theory, being highly abstract, cannot really guide the party leader in deciding how positively or negatively he is to judge any phenomenon at any particular time. After all, Marx and Engels themselves did not always agree on such appraisals.

This ambivalence is intensified by the fact that the communist thinks on several levels of abstraction at one and the same time. Not only that, he or she must plan the course of action on several different levels—maximum and minimum programs, strategy and tactics, action based on principles as against that which is an accommodation to special circumstances, action in different locales. Obviously, various courses of action are open to the party in any one situation, all of them fully consonant with Marxist-Leninist theory.

To prevent paralysis or chaos, therefore, more than theoretical skills (consciousness) is required. According to Lenin's principles, consciousness must be linked to an efficient decision-making machinery so as to make sure that in every case the correct decision is made. And that for every situation there is one and only one correct decision Lenin was convinced, even though it seems, in the light of what we have discussed above, this conviction cannot be reconciled with the ambivalent (dialectical) and multilevel approach to reality characterizing Marxism. To be sure, Marx and Engels themselves, however prone they were on the basis of their method to regard the world in contradictory terms, were often as dogmatic as Lenin when discussing courses of action. In their cases, too, we get the impression that they recognized only one solution to a problem as correct.

Lenin, moreover, was a rare type of revolutionary: a revolutionary with a bureaucratic mind. Such a combination is rare because most revolutionaries so hate the bureaucracy of the social system they want to overthrow that they come to hate all official-dom. Certainly, in the political thought of Western liberalism, which is suspicious of all governmental authority, this is true, and Marxism, being an heir to the liberal heritage, shares its anti-bureaucratic bias in the main. Lenin, however, as a rule did not share it. He seems to have felt that there was something inherently rational in good bureaucratic organization; that such organization, when put to work, would produce correct decisions, especially when it consisted of conscious people. It may very well be that this faith in rational organization only covered up his desire to create a governmental apparatus completely subservient to him; perhaps he was organization-happy because it suited his purposes. I for one believe that this is part of the truth. Yet it is true also that Lenin's preoccupation with principles and problems of centralized bureaucratic organization is in tune with the beliefs and preconceptions of Marx and Engels. After all, as prophets of the cult of rationality and the good life in this world, they praised not only the machine age but also collectivism and large-scale, centralized administration. In their eyes, these were aspects of up-to-date civilization, and they would be preserved and fostered in the socialist society.* To this one must add that Lenin's entire schooling in Marxism and Marxist party politics came from the leading Marxist party of the late nineteenth century, the German Social-Democratic Party. It is from this party, the first modern mass party and an important pioneer of political mass organization, that Lenin learned the organizational principles he imposed on his branch of the Russian movement. Still, Lenin's motivation is rather irrelevant. What does matter, for the history and development of communism, are the principles of organization that emerged.

Lenin wanted the party to be a striking organization which could be totally committed to any action as quickly as possible. He wanted this organization to be absolutely centralized and subject to firm control by its leaders. He wanted its organization to be hierarchical, following the command principle of armed forces, where the chief virtue of the lower ranks is discipline and obedience. Comparison of the party with a military organization is not a far-fetched idea attributable to Western critics. On the contrary, Lenin made it clear that military organization was the pattern according to which he wished the party to be organized. Communist ideologists have a predilection for military terminology. The revolutions they promote are battles to be fought and won; the societies within which they occur are fronts in a global war; the workers are the rank-and-file soldiers; other classes furnish

---

*If I have drawn a contradictory picture of Marxist attitudes toward bureaucracy, I have done so in the awareness that one must not expect political philosophies to be altogether consistent.

reserve troops; and the party is the general staff.

But the conception of the party as a disciplined bureaucratic body was in sharp conflict with another principle of organization: the democratic one. That the proletarian movement should organize itself and manage its own affairs democratically follows logically from the assumption that the proletariat is conscious. And if that assumption is replaced by one that attributes consciousness only to the party elite, then democracy should reign within that vanguard of the elect. For surely, where everyone is conscious, everyone's voice should be heard, and everyone's counsel is of equal worth. Not even Lenin ever saw fit to repudiate this argument.

Bureaucratic-authoritarian principles of organization thus were in conflict with democratic ones. Lenin attempted to resolve this clash by a formula: The party, he argued, should be governed in accordance with the principle of "democratic centralism."

The formula symbolizes the desire to merge both principles. According to Lenin, party policies should be formulated by absolutely free discussion and deliberation, with every party member entitled to participate either directly or through freely elected representatives. The formal structure of the party corresponds to this, in that the sovereign body which, in theory, determines policy is the party congress of delegates representing the entire membership. All executive organizations of the party, such as the Central Committee and its numerous subsidiary or servant organizations, are formally accountable to the congress. In addition to providing for free discussion of all pending questions, the democratic element of democratic centralism was meant to give each individual party member freedom to criticize. Indeed, Lenin once defined democratic centralism as "freedom to criticize and unity in action." The centralistic principle of "unity in action" was to prevail only after policies had been adopted and had become party law. Then, after every member had had his or her opportunity to speak up, all dissent was to be suppressed and the party was to display monolithic unity. Any sign of disagreement at such a time was to be regarded as a breach of discipline and punished by expulsion. A party committed in action could not tolerate dissenters within its ranks.

Thus freedom to criticize was obviously to be sharply circumscribed. But exactly how to circumscribe it remained a problem.

To be legitimate, said the party leaders, criticism should be constructive. But what is the criterion of constructiveness? Criticism, said the party rules, should focus on the execution of adopted policies rather than on the policies themselves. *What* was being done should be beyond criticism; only *how* it was being done could be a matter of dispute. But the borderline between policy formulation and policy execution does not exist except in textbooks. In practice it is meaningless. Moreover, who is to have the right to challenge policies that have been in force for a long time, or for any length of time? Somebody must be able to point out that circumstances have changed and that measures once adopted unanimously have outlived their usefulness. Someone must be authorized to prepare agendas for meetings and congresses and thereby indicate what problems deserve to be discussed. But according to the rules of centralism and discipline, such suggestions ought not to be made by any member while the party is committed in action. Yet, is not the party always committed? Is there ever a moment when dissent is not dangerous and a breach of discipline and unanimity?

In reality, the cards were stacked overwhelmingly against democratic principles. Lenin may have paid lip service to them; he may even have been completely sincere in his praises of party democracy. But he was also highly impatient with criticism and dissent. He was contemptuous or perhaps even fearful of Russian intellectuals and their proverbial knack for interminable and aimless discussion. He wanted action rather than words, results instead of dreams. And to attain these aims he favored centralism and authoritarianism.

In addition to Lenin's tremendous prestige within the party, two devices became important in curbing democracy. One was a rule outlawing "factionalism," adopted at the Tenth Congress of the Russian Communist party in 1921, which had the effect of atomizing all dissent. Disagreement and criticism could still be voiced, but it had to be voiced by individuals. The formation of dissenting groups, the writing of minority reports or rival platforms, even the organization of minority discussion groups were outlawed as treason against the party. These formal curbs on the freedom of discussion were supplemented by an increasing tendency on the part of the leaders to control the membership through the party's administrative organs, to make the representative gatherings more and more subservient to the party bureaucracy, to pack them with yes men and women, and the like. Centralism consequently won a complete victory over party democracy. This was true of the Russian Communist party and, for a long time, also the communist parties throughout the world. But, for reasons to be discussed later in this book, it is no longer true today.

WORLD VIEW

The composite picture of the communists as Lenin himself visualized them, is that of radical, revolutionary Marxists imbued with loathing for capitalism and yearning for socialism, and in a hurry to attain their goal; ruthless in their methods and opportunistic (Lenin would have said flexible) in their strategies; absolutely loyal to their party and its leaders, and filled with holy intolerance of any ideas or even facts that might shake their loyalty; intolerant also of any political leaders, especially those calling themselves socialist or communist, not in total agreement with the party; and ever eager to deepen their own consciousness, yet disciplined and obedient as party servants. When Lenin talked about "hard" Marxists or "hard" Bolsheviks, he had in mind that combination of determination and devotion, lack of squeamishness, adaptability, and loyalty. As we shall see when discussing the history of the party, he did not always get the kind of following he wanted; the party also, at various times, attracted people who had some, but not all, of the desired traits. (The picture is complicated further by the fact that the kinds of virtue that Lenin demanded of his disciples after the party acquired political power are significantly different from those of the model revolutionary.) The ideal Bolsheviks, however, are foremost "hard" and radical—a simple syndrome of traits which distinguishes them from adherents of most other parties of either the right or the left. To make the image more complete we shall have to describe their general world view. By that I mean not their philosophy but their image of society in the twentieth century. To the communist, ours is the age of *imperialism*; in order to understand what this implies, we should determine what the term *imperialism* means in communist writings. For this purpose, we shall have to begin by sketching the circumstances under which the term gained currency.

The word began to be used around the beginning of our century, when the expansion of the European powers into economically "backward" and politically defenseless areas of Asia and Africa had reached its peak. New colonial empires were established at that time, spheres of influence and domination were carved out, and fierce rivalries developed between the European powers in their competition for areas of domination.

For the Western world in general, this was a period of rapid economic growth through the work of ever-larger industrial and financial corporate structures, of quickly rising living standards, and increasing national consciousness. For the Marxist movement, it was a time of puzzlement and soul searching, because so many features of the contemporary world corresponded less and less with the Marxist model as its members understood it. The decline of capitalism seemed remoter than ever. The revolutionary spirit of the working class was yielding to the tendency to strive for reforms within the existing system. The entire timetable of Marxism seemed hopelessly upset. Where the spirit of revolution was still alive, it was in relatively "backward" countries, in which proletarian revolutions did not make much sense according to a strict and dogmatic reading of Marxism. All these developments required explanation, and the communist theory of imperialism was an attempt to provide it.

Reduced to the simplest terms, this explanation runs as follows: Instead of having developed its internal contradictions and tensions to a point where a revolutionary break must occur, capitalism has found a way out of these contradictions, even though they were previously thought to be insoluble. The way out is expansion throughout the world in search of cheap raw materials, ready markets for commodities and for excess capital, and, most important, cheap labor that can be exploited in unprecedented measure. This expansion of capitalism is called imperialism.

In his attempt to describe the social processes going on in his time, Lenin further defined imperialism. He described it as an intensification of all those features that Marx and Engels had attributed to capitalism. In his law of the concentration of capital, Marx had described how the small entrepreneur is inevitably wiped out by larger competitors and capital is concentrated in fewer and fewer hands. According to communist theory, this concentration has proceeded apace and has led to the development of *monopoly capitalism.* Similarly, the fate Marx and Engels predicted for the majority of the middle classes, namely, transformation into proletarians, has, according to Lenin, become reality; almost everyone outside a small power elite is a helpless cog in a vast commercialized machine dominated by monopolists.

But if indeed the tendencies seen by the writers of the *Communist Manifesto* have reached their peak, what is to explain the failure of the revolutionary movement and the staying power of capitalism? The communists' reply is that this intensification of various essential features of capitalism has temporarily eased some of the strains under which the system labored. First of all, the reign of monopoly and the increasing interference of centralized government in the economy reduce the anarchy which, according to Marx and Engels, characterized free-enterprise economy. Monopoly capitalism and state capitalism, as the communists call the modern Western systems, are guided and planned. Further, they argue, monopoly has grown so strong in its grip on the system that it can afford to make political concessions to the lower classes and thus tie them more firmly to the status quo. Moreover, monopoly capitalism, by exploiting "backward" areas, reaps such enormous profits—communist theory calls them superprofits—that it can bribe the proletariat (or at least its leaders) also with economic concessions, that is, with a rising standard of living. One of the fundamental laws of capitalist development in Marxist theory, the law of the increasing misery of the masses, is thus substantially modified. Finally, the workers have been corrupted also by the fierce nationalism that, as a result of imperialist competition, has been fostered within each imperialist nation. This nationalism, to which according to Lenin the working-class leadership especially has fallen victim, has corroded international proletarian solidarity and made the workers' movement a pawn in the hands of the ruling classes.

The chances for a proletarian revolution therefore seem more remote than ever. But communist theory resurrects the optimism of Marx and Engels by uncovering new tendencies toward the eventual breakdown of capitalism and new revolutionary forces to speed up the process and carry it forward to construct a socialist commonwealth. This new theory of doom and renascence forms the core of the theory of imperialism.

According to communist thought, the "contradictions" of capitalism have been overcome within the Western nations only to reappear on a global scale. Within any one nation, the anarchy of capitalist production may have been reduced to a minimum. But sharp and deadly competition lives on between international monopolies and between the various imperialist nations, and on a global level capitalism is therefore an anarchic as ever. Analyzing this competition in some detail, Lenin came to the conclusion that it could be resolved only by war, and the inevitability of imperialist wars, that is, wars between various capitalist nations, remained an axiom of communist theory until very recently, even though the course of world history since 1917 had given rise to the nagging fear that a countertendency might exist: Ever since the birth of a communist regime in Russia, communist leaders have ever been in fear of a world-wide alliance of all imperialist nations in a crusade to wipe out Soviet Russia. For several decades this fear of an all-imperialist bloc and of "capitalist encirclement" played an important role in communist ideology.

Further contradictions of capitalism are seen in imperialism. For instance, capitalism, according to communist theory, has saved itself from collapse by exporting capital into underdeveloped areas. But, as industrial civilization engulfs the entire globe, it becomes more and more difficult to dispose of the faster and faster accumulating surpluses. Soon there will be no new frontiers nor safety valves. Moreover, by exporting capital, the West also exports capital*ism* with all its stresses and its inherent revolutionary potential to areas hitherto untouched by Western history. Not only competition but also those other features Marx had seen in capitalism—exploitation and domination and a resulting struggle of classes—reappear on a global scale. The new class struggle that develops in the age of imperialism, according to communist theory, is more complicated than the conflict between capitalists and proletarians was in the nineteenth century. The old struggle persists, although it is mitigated temporarily in the imperialist countries. And it now goes on everywhere, even if only under the surface. In addition, however, world society is now divided into the exploiters and the exploited in yet another fashion: The new exploited populations are entire nations, namely, those "backward," underdeveloped nations on whom the capitalist world has been encroaching. Modern communist theory attributes to them the same relationship to the exploiter nations as the proletariat was to have to the bourgeoisie. The class struggle is thus partly transformed into an international conflict.

This picture, which has been drawn in very simplified strokes, has interesting implications for the overall theory of revolution of Marx and Engels. One concept that was very important to their earlier followers was that of *maturity:* Conditions had to be ripe for a proletarian revolution before working-class action made sense; capitalism had to be highly developed as a social system, and industrial technology had to be sufficiently advanced to provide a decent livelihood for all. Then conditions would be mature for the proletarian revolution. Now this concept is virtually turned upside down. Industrial capitalism and the revolutionary movement are seen as developing not in direct but in inverse proportion to each other. Highly developed industrial countries get stuck in the rut of imperialism, while the revolution develops in less developed countries. *Consciousness is more important than the maturity of conditions.* This is one of the implications of the communist theory of imperialism.

Another implication is the theory of "combined development." The sharp line drawn above between exploiter nations and exploited nations does not imply that either type is homogeneous. To be sure, in the imperialist world the class struggle may be stifled, but it is taken for granted by most (not all) communists that eventually it will erupt with renewed vigor. Meanwhile in the underdeveloped nations a far more complicated class conflict rages. For in these societies the fight of the proletariat against the bourgeoisie goes on simultaneously with the struggle of peasants against landlords, bourgeois against traditional rulers, caste against caste, nationality against nationality. Thus backward societies, in the communist view, combine features that in the West characterized different stages of development. Noncontemporaneous elements here are telescoped so as to coincide in time, because modern civilization, through Western imperialism, has been superimposed on societies hitherto untouched by Western developments.

To the revolutionary strategist this phenomenon opens up exciting new perspectives for action. It makes possible unique combinations of social forces; it creates political constellations of new and ever-shifting character, which have to be examined anew in each country. And this necessity to regard every underdeveloped country as unique in its social problems gives theoretical justification to all the pragmatism and seeming opportunism of communist parties. The strategies and tactics used by Marx and Engels, which used to be copied slavishly by their earlier followers, have ceased to be obligatory.

Not only do strategies and tactics become more flexible on the basis of such theories, however; the whole conception of the revolution changes profoundly. First of all, in the communist view, the revolution is no longer to be carried out by the proletariat alone but by an alliance of the Western proletariat with the underdeveloped nations and the colonies and dependencies. Its point of departure, its origin, is no longer the condition of the working class but the condition of all humanity, seen as victims of imperialism. The crucial point of Marxism, that conditions have to be ripe for revolution, has been amended, as we have seen. The maturity of capitalism now is seen to lead to revolution, not in the capitalist world, but somewhere else. The aims of the revolution also have changed. In the *Communist Manifesto*, the proletariat was to seize the means of industrial production in the name of society and utilize them in collectivist fashion for the benefit of all. The aim of the new revolution must be different, for in underdeveloped areas there is little that can be seized, and current means of production will not suffice to satisfy the material needs of those societies. The revolution of the colonial world has as its immediate aim the destruction of imperialism. It is to weaken the rule of capital not only in the colonies but also in the home countries by knocking the props from underneath the tottering system. Having accomplished this negative task, the coming world revolution is to proceed toward an even more difficult undertaking, which is to *build* modern industrial civilization in the underdeveloped areas, to copy the achievements of the capitalist West, in order to emancipate all peoples from it. For this, strong communist governments are required; hence it would be foolish to expect that the revolution will lead at once to the withering away of oppressive institutions. On the contrary, the emerging communist states will have to emphasize dictatorship, sacrifice, and continued alienation, for entire nations will have to be reeducated to be made fit for the machine age. In this fashion, the revolution, which in the minds of Marx and Engels was to have been a comparatively brief interlude, albeit violent and bloody, now assumes much greater dimensions in time by becoming an entire era of what communists call "socialist construction." Communism thus has turned into an ideology of modernization, and communist societies must be defined primarily as massive attempts at rapid economic and cultural development. We will develop some implications of these ideas in the chapters dealing with Third World Communism; but, since Russia can be regarded as belonging to both Europe and Asia, and therefore as both a practitioner and a victim of Western imperialism, the transformation of Marxism from a Western into an anti-Western ideology can be observed quite clearly in the Russian Revolution, to which we will now turn.

CHAPTER 5

The Russian Revolution, 1917–1938

Marxism entered the Third World because it was a convenient framework for combining a modernizing movement with a sharp rejection of Western domination. One could argue that it had been adopted by Russian revolutionaries for similar reasons. Radicals in tsarist Russia were in agreement that tsarism had to be replaced by a more democratic system, but they sharply disagreed over all questions related to the implementation of this goal. The Bolshevik answers to these questions have been summarized in Chapter 4. However, the Bolsheviks were only one of several radical parties active in the Russian Empire during its last three decades.

In early 1917 the tsarist system collapsed. Russia at that time was in the third year of World War I. Casualties had been high; vast territories were under enemy occupation; the country's economy was in shambles. The fall of the tsar and the disappearance of his entire administrative structure came at a time when Russia was faced with urgent problems, and the sudden loss of leaders made the people all the more eager and desperate for quick solutions to the questions concerning war and peace, questions concerning property distribution, and the forms of government that should now be created. In situations of this sort, when authority has disappeared but people desperately want some problems solved, the leadership proposing the quickest and most radical solutions is likely to gain a large following, while those who hesitate will be swept aside. Lenin, sensing the desperation of large masses of the population, rode to power by echoing their fears and hopes. While he was aware that endorsing some of their demands had little to do with the historic scenario that Marxism had envisioned, he argued that his party could not forego seizing power when it was there to be seized, and while he also knew that Russian society was not ripe for socialism the way Marxist theory had proposed, he justified the seizure of power in Russia by assuming that a communist revolution in that underdeveloped country would cause a global chain reaction of revolutions, especially in Central and Western Europe. Thus on November 7, 1917, the first communist regime of modern times was born in Russia.

In short, Lenin from the very beginning was unwilling to regard the overthrow of tsarism as an end in itself or even as a major achievement giving time to pause. Instead, he saw it as a mere beginning, a prologue to further revolutionary events, an opportunity for quick advances, and he was eager to get done with the further tasks as quickly as possible. In advancing such ideas, he was at first far ahead of most of his closest friends and associates. They were unprepared for, and frightened by, his sweeping program and sought to prevent or soften what they thought would be rash, adventurous actions. Some, like Stalin, rallied around Lenin after a while. Others became ever more alarmed. Their conflict with Lenin came to a head in October of 1917, when, from his Finnish hiding place, he bombarded the Central Committee with messages urging them to prepare an armed uprising at once with the aim of overthrowing the provisional government and establishing a Soviet regime. Two of his closest associates, Zinoviev and Kamenev, publicly dissociated themselves from such a course of action and were virtually read out of the party by Lenin. Yet they had done little more than express openly the doubts shared by many of their comrades.

Once the Bolsheviks had seized power in the name of the Soviet (at that time they were in the majority in this body), the heterogeneity of party leadership and the prevalence of open debate within this group were intensified by the fact that the first few years of communist rule brought acute problems that no one had anticipated. Crises can unify the group they confront, but they can also have divisive effects; the grave problems faced by the party in the first few years of its rule did both.

At the root of the problems was the fact that the Communist party had come to power with the firm expectation that this event would produce a world-wide chain reaction of proletarian revolutions; this world revolution in turn would ensure the immediate advent of socialism, even in Russia. It took only a few months of Soviet rule to convince at least Lenin that these ideals were not going to be attained immediately. With the gradual ebbing of hopes for a general European revolution, his government was forced not only to think of its own preservation but also to postpone the Good Society as far as domestic measures were concerned. The grim fight for survival in the civil war that broke out in the summer of 1918 required the abandonment of democratic ideals and the imposition in their stead of strict military discipline; the economic ruin following in its wake forced Lenin to take the most stringent measures to save his regime from collapse. Moreover, it dawned on the communist leaders that the vigor with which substantial portions of the lower-class population of Russia had fought for the Revolution did not necessarily imply that they were in general on a high level of literacy, education, or productivity. On the contrary, the human material at the disposal of the party was on an abysmally low cultural level—hardly the basis for the ideal communist society.

Some of the repressive measures taken during the civil war were defended by many communists as attempts to create immediately the communist or socialist society. Each new measure of nationalization and centralization, each new tightening of controls, was praised as the harbinger of true socialism. But other members of the party saw in these steps a betrayal of the ideas for which they had fought, and Lenin had to impose every such measure against vigorous opposition from leading party members. The ideas of 1917 thus served both to justify the civil-war measures (known in the history books as ''war communism'') by stirring expectations of the immediate attainment of socialism and to criticize them as a violation of communist ideals. It appeared that Lenin's left-wing followers, who had been the most sanguine in their expectations in 1917, tended to be the most critical of war communism and simultaneously to harbor the greatest illusions about its results. In contrast, the old-time Leninists, who had resisted their leader in 1917, were less burdened with idealistic hopes and with squeamishness. Consequently, war communism did not present them with such acute ideological problems.

Once the civil war was won, the party, in a sudden about-face, made substantial concessions to free enterprise and other capitalist features; once again the membership was jolted and perturbed, and many of them retained serious misgivings about the new policies, which they regarded as a retreat from socialist principles. These heated debates, in the course of which Lenin was outvoted more than once in the Central Committee, prompted him to curb dissent and discussion within the party by the measures described above and by such devices as control over recruitment, assignments, and other personnel policies. Because of these steps to silence dissenting members, the doubts arising over the concessions made after the end of the civil war remained unexpressed in the main while Lenin was still alive. But they were to erupt all the more forcefully when illness and death removed him from the scene and the curtain rose on a new act in the history of Russian communism.

This sketch of the history of the Russian Communist party can, of course, offer no more than a few highlights of an involved and complex development. In summary: The party grew up as a tightly organized and self-conscious faction within the Russian Social-Democratic Labor party; it strove to gain full control over the Russian working-class movement with the aim of making its own policies prevail, and its leader did everything within his power to make it into an organization whose every move was well under his own control, rejecting and casting out all persons and groups who refused to submit to such control.

After the Revolution, the effort to convert the working-class movement into an efficient and tightly controlled political machine (in Russian: *apparat*) was extended to the international working-class movement. On the basis of plans Lenin had conceived during World War I, he created an international league of communist parties, the Third, or Communist, International, the bylaws of which were drafted so as to resemble closely those of the Russian party and to give control over membership and policies of all its constituent parties to Lenin and his Russian colleagues. The Communist International, with its numerous auxiliary organizations, thus quickly became a global extension of the Russian *apparat*.

Yet when Lenin became ill, the problems of party policy, organization, and personnel were by no means solved. A number of fundamental differences in attitude divided the party along policy lines. The resulting formation of factions was complicated by personal antagonisms and friendships between different groups of leaders. Finally, the death of the leader, in whose hands most lines of control and command had been concentrated, brought out serious unresolved problems of party government and precipitated a deep and prolonged crisis within the party.

PHASES OF SOVIET RULE

One thing that will emerge from this chapter is the changing nature of the Soviet regime. Its basic aims and activities, its institutions and the entire social structure beneath these institutions, have several times undergone radical transformations. Hence to speak about *the* Soviet government or *the* Soviet society is misleading, since there has been a succession of markedly distinct social and political systems. To be sure, there are continuities within this recurrent change. From its beginnings to our day, the Soviet Union has been ruled by one and the same political party. This ruling party has continually expressed its allegiance to one and the same official doctrine. Hence there has been political and ideological continuity. I would argue, however, that these continuities are formal rather than real. For one thing, the membership and organization of the party, as well as its place and functions within Soviet society, have changed as much as the society itself; further, although the words of Marxism-Leninism rarely change, the meaning given to them, and the relationship between doctrine and politics, has not remained the same, as I shall try to show.*

The Bolsheviks expected their revolution to result in a worldwide chain reaction of proletarian revolutions, which, they assumed, would ensure the birth of a global (or at least all-European) socialist commonwealth. The kind of socialist commonwealth Lenin envisaged is described in some detail in his unfinished *The State and Revolution*, which he wrote in the fall of

*For an elaboration of my argument about the changing nature of Soviet society, see my chapter "The Soviet Political System" in Samuel Hendel and Randolph L. Braham, *USSR Fifty Years Later: The Promise and the Reality* (New York, 1967).

1917 and which echoed sentiments widespread in his party at the time. In it he visualized that the creation of a Soviet state would at once lead to the expropriation of capitalists and landowners and therefore to the abolition of commodity production (i.e., production for the market). It would lead to classless society, in which the material wants of all could be fully satisfied. Since by working for the common good all members of society would be working directly for themselves, they would, Lenin foresaw, gladly give their energies for production; no longer would there be incentive problems. Moreover, the need for people to dominate or exploit other people would disappear, and hence institutions of coercion and government, such as armies, police forces, courts, and bureaucracies, would disappear. The people would manage their communal affairs spontaneously, directly, rationally. The administration of the industrial establishment, in turn, would be reduced to simple tasks of accounting and controlling, tasks so simple that they could be performed by anyone. Since these would be all the "governmental" tasks remaining to be done, any "female cook" could run the government, and administrative responsibilities could therefore be rotated among all.

These sanguine expectations held by the Bolsheviks in the last months of 1917 were not merely propaganda designed to justify their seizure of power. On the contrary, the Bolsheviks were convinced that this ideal society was within reach, and it took some of them years to shed such beliefs. Since then, the blueprint Lenin provided for a classless and stateless society has become a source of embarrassment to the party, a symbol of unfulfilled dreams or broken promises, an idealistic mirror that mocked the face of an exceedingly drab reality.*

For many Marxists looking at the Russian Revolution with the wisdom of hindsight, the Bolshevik takeover in the October Revolution is an event that should not have taken place because Russia was not ripe for socialism then, and as a consequence of

---

*Although Lenin's book on *The State and Revolution* is often assigned to students to acquaint them with the writings of Lenin, I should like to stress its unrepresentative nature. I should go so far as to say that it is the most unrepresentative, the most atypical work of all that Lenin has produced; it is an aberration from his customary thought pattern. See Robert V. Daniels, "The State and Revolution: A Case Study in the Genesis and Transformation of Communist Ideology," in *The American Slavic and East European Review*, 12 (February 1953): 22–43.

this premature revolution, the Soviet Union has turned into a caricature of what Marx, Engels, and their earlier followers had envisaged.*

For developments took a different turn. The workers of the West did not take up the cue tossed them by the Russian Revolution. The Bolshevik regime of Russia remained isolated and harassed. Within the country, a protracted and bitter civil war broke out, and in the narrow territory remaining under Soviet rule uncooperative, hostile elements abounded. The regime truly had its back to the wall. It won the civil war partly because substantial sections of the peasantry and the national minorities joined the workers in supporting the regime actively or passively, or at least showed themselves more hostile to the counterrevolutionary forces than to the Red Army, and partly because the Bolsheviks adopted stringent emergency measures to keep themselves in power. They imposed the strictest military discipline on the entire population, including their own supporters and party members. Like commandants of a besieged fortress, they commandeered every ounce of available human and material resources for the civil-war effort, disdaining neither to rob the peasants of their produce by force nor to employ tsarist officers, capitalist entrepreneurs, and other "bourgeois specialists." Ruling by stark terror, with the support at times of ignorant and dissolute mobs who often abused the power so suddenly thrust upon them, smashing existing institutions and assigning loyal revolutionaries to administrative jobs for which they were altogether unprepared, improvising and fumbling, they yet found this to be the time for brave cultural experiments in many fields, most of them based on the notion that the "brotherhood of all men" was about to become reality. Antagonizing countless supporters, they yet managed to inspire an entire generation of Russian youngsters with heaven-storming enthusiasm, with the readiness to sacrifice everything to the building of a world without exploitation and inequality, a socialist commonwealth that would begin as soon as the civil war would be won. This was the heroic period of the Russian Revolution, usually referred to as the period of war com-

---

*For a recent statement making this point, see Felipa Garcia Casals, *The Syncretic Society* (White Plains, N.Y.: M.E. Sharpe, 1980).

munism, a period in which all the worst fears of antirevolutionary people in Russia and in the West were confirmed by the excesses of the Red Terror, the insolence of drunken or ragged proletarians, and the muddle of communist bureaucracy, while the image that Soviet Russia presented to her sympathizers abroad was still one of unsullied revolutionary pioneering.

Yet the ruthlessness of the civil-war emergency measures exhausted the credit of the Bolshevik regime among many of its supporters. By the time the civil war was won, the regime was therefore close to political collapse. In addition, seven years of foreign and civil war had brought unspeakable economic ruin to the country. Drastic measures were required to restore the economy and pacify at least parts of the population. The measures adopted for the purpose are known as the New Economic Policy, or NEP. They consisted of the reintroduction of private enterprise in agriculture, trade, crafts, and small manufacture, with only foreign trade, major industries, and political rule remaining firmly in the hands of the party and its government. (Concessions made to Western business firms allowing them to exploit Soviet resources or build up manufacturing enterprises made no serious dent in these monopolies.)

The NEP meant a relaxation of Bolshevik terror. Members of the old ruling classes remained disfranchised and discriminated against, but they were at least permitted to make a living. Workers still enjoyed privileges over the members of other classes, but economically the NEP benefited well-to-do peasants and small businessmen. Bold experiments were still conducted by the party in various cultural fields, but other currents in art, literature, science, and mores were at least tolerated. To the average Soviet citizen looking back to this period in the 1930s or 1940s, the years of the NEP must have appeared like a veritable golden age. After the hardships of the heroic period, normalcy seemed to have returned.

Yet this normalcy did not look attractive to many members of the Communist party. To be sure, they had adopted the NEP as a necessary retreat; they had said, with Lenin, that they were accepting it "seriously and for a long time," but nonetheless not all had accepted it gladly. True, most party members had had enough of civil war, terror, and heroism for a while. But not all were comfortable in the humdrum tasks of gradual economic reconstruction and of teaching illiterates the ABC's or with the tolerance shown to peasants, small businessmen, and foreign concessionaires. The men at the head of the party had spent their lives in an agonizing struggle for a lofty goal. Most of them could not possibly be satisfied unless there was a chance to make that goal—socialism—reality.

Conflicting schools of thought developed within the Russian Communist party concerning the manner in which socialism might be made to come about. One group, usually considered to be the right wing of the party, developed an almost Fabian theory of inevitable gradualness, based on thoughts expressed in Lenin's last articles and speeches. They held that the uneasy compromise between socialism and free enterprise would give way to pure socialism in the course of a slow, organic evolution and that in similar fashion the social basis of the regime, that is, the "alliance" between workers and peasants, would gradually "grow over" into a purely proletarian society. The economic transformation, entailing the gradual waning of free enterprise and other capitalist features, would come about as the result of free competition between capitalism and socialism, and not through coercion or governmental arbitrariness. The most outspoken among them therefore argued that the free-enterprise features of the NEP ought to be fostered and encouraged rather than curbed. Precisely the free unfolding of capitalism—perhaps with constitutional democracy added—would hasten the growth of socialism. The party's chief role in this process, they tended to think, was that of promoting the cultural revolution, that is, the transformation, by education, of Russia's ignorant, backward masses into informed, sophisticated, responsible citizens. The cultural revolution, they thought, was the most essential prerequisite and the surest guarantee of the eventual victory of socialism over capitalism.

The people who developed gradualist views were of different types. The chief theoreticians of gradualism appear to have been antitotalitarian idealists such as N. N. Bukharin, who in the period of war communism (if not before) had become suspicious of violent and authoritarian methods. In their attempts to provide their political views with ideological support, they interpreted Marxism in strictly determinist fashion, leading to the conclusion that it is impossible to go against economic laws or to skip historically predetermined stages of development, and that it would be foolish or criminal to attempt it. Similarly, Marxist dialectics was transformed by Bukharin into a theory of equilibrium that supported his reluctance to engage in daring and radical political experiments. Theoreticians such as he were supported by a host of party bureaucrats who seemed loath to jeopardize the interests of their political machine for the sake of bold new adventures, people whose vested interest in the existing system made them timid if not conservative.

Against the gradualists stood those party leaders who argued that the NEP was a danger that must be overcome by daring measures. It was a political danger because the dominating position taken in the national economy by the successful peasant and small businessperson sooner or later would be transformed into political dominance, so that the proletarian regime was in danger of being swamped by the petty bourgeoisie. Economically the NEP was dangerous, they held, because Soviet Russia was threatened with the prospect of getting stuck in economic backwardness. Socialism, they argued, was possible only in a modern industrial society; the first task of the communist regime would therefore have to be to erect a modern industrial structure.

The spokespeople for the left wing of the Russian Communist party—outstanding among them were Leon Trotsky and Eugene Preobrazhenski—gave dramatic emphasis to their theory by calling for a policy of *primitive* (or *primary*) *socialist accumulation*. Primary accumulation, in Marxist theory, is that sanguinary process of robbery, piracy, conquest, extortion, and other violent means through which society accumulates the material resources and "free" labor that enable the capitalist mode of production to develop. In the words of Marx, it is "an accumulation not the result of the capitalist mode of production, but its starting point"; he adds that it "plays in Political Economy about the same part as original sin in theology."[*] Marx describes it with loathing and moral indignation, concluding that capitalism comes into the world "dripping from head to foot, from every pore, with blood and dirt."[†] This then was the image Trotsky and Preobrazhenski evoked in demanding a policy of primitive socialist accumula-

[*]*Capital* (Chicago, 1906), I, p. 784.
[†]*Ibid.*, I, p. 834.

tion. They argued that just as capitalism could arise only after surplus wealth and a surplus population had been accumulated, so the creation of an industrial base was the essential prerequisite for building socialism. In addition, industrialization was the only policy that could prevent the revolution from being overwhelmed by peasants and NEP people (small businesspeople). They warned that the policy they were advocating would require harsh measures and dictatorial discipline. The resources to be invested in industrialization would have to be provided by Russia's population through forced savings. And yet they argued that the task could be accomplished without living standards falling drastically and without a renewal of the Red Terror of civil-war days. Whatever the measures and the methods, however, the revolution would be lost if it did not industrialize.

On the very left wing of the party, there were small groups of leaders who argued that the Revolution had already been lost or betrayed, that it had followed a cycle similar to that of the French Revolution, in which the radical Jacobin dreams of equality and justice had been destroyed by the Thermidorian reaction and the ensuing Bonapartist dictatorship. According to such men as Shliapnikov and Sapronov, leaders of the ultraleftist opposition, the ideals of 1917 had been betrayed by the Communist party itself. Instead of socialism, a mixture of capitalist free enterprise and industrial dictatorship had been set up, they argued; instead of proletarian rule, rule by the party, and not even the entire party at that, but only the handful of leaders constituting the core of the Old Guard. These people, ardently committed to the anarcho-syndicalist dreams of 1917, ultimately came to the conclusion that a third revolution (third after the two revolutions of February and October of 1917) was needed, this one to be a genuine proletarian revolution to overthrow the dictatorship of the party and to establish a genuine socialist workers' democracy.

As we shall see, these divergent views concerning the most desirable or necessary development of the Russian Revolution were linked with equally conflicting policy lines concerning the policies of the international communist movement. Disputes over policy and ultimate goals, moreover, led to discussions in virtually every other field of learning, thought, and action; and the 1920s, more than any other period, therefore witnessed a thorough and highly controversial reexamination of Marxism and Leninism in all its details, a debate that was far more open than any similar disputes within the party were later allowed to be. For the student of communist political systems anywhere, it is interesting and important to study these debates because similar problems are likely to trouble any communist regime arising in an underdeveloped country. Communist experience in Eastern Europe and East Asia can thus be regarded as a series of variations on themes struck some decades ago by Soviet Russia.

The differences of opinion over the further development of the revolution began to plague the party soon after the beginning of the NEP. They were quite heated in the last year of Lenin's life and became extremely bitter after his death, which added the fuel of an intense power struggle to the fire of ideological arguments. Not only opinions but personalities and ambitions, too, clashed head-on, and the conflict split the party into hardly reconcilable factions. By *party* we mean that small group of Old Guard leaders who as members of its highest policy-making and administrative bodies were in actual command of the party. Even before Lenin was dead, maneuvering began in this high command to settle the succession problem. Interest centered on the role and personality of Trotsky, who in the minds of many people outside and inside the party was the heir apparent. Although he had for many years opposed Lenin and his Bolshevik faction and joined them only in the summer of 1917, it was he who had been the chief tactician of the Bolshevik seizure of power, creator of the Red Army and main strategist of the civil war, savior of Leningrad, and second in prestige only to Lenin himself. Abroad, it was customary to mention Lenin and Trotsky in the same breath as the two-man team ruling Soviet Russia. Within the party, however, there were many leaders who well remembered Trotsky's ancient conflicts with the Bolsheviks and the comparatively recent vintage of his party membership. To be sure, in joining he had brought with him a bevy of friends who at once became prominent leaders under Lenin and could support Trotsky from positions of strength within the party. But against this faithful cohort stood a broad stratum of old associates of the dead leader who deeply resented the newcomer's prestige and power.

Trotsky's own personality was not designed to help him win his colleagues' favor. The brilliance of his mind, his pen, and his oratory was matched by great arrogance and tactlessness, by a certain inability to deal with people and to recognize political constellations within the party. As a political manipulator he was no match for the old Leninist organizers; after a few years of bitter struggle that badly divided the party, Trotsky and his allies had been outmaneuvered and were then eliminated from the party. In the course of these struggles, some party leaders who had at first supported Stalin but had then thrown their support to Trotsky were thrown out of the party also. Stalin gained supremacy because the whole strength of the party organization was in his hands, and as General Secretary he wielded that strength skillfully.

Once he was well in control, he adopted a great deal of the program of his left-wing critics and, as a consequence, faced new opposition, this time from those who had been his closest allies in the struggle against Trotsky—theoreticians like Bukharin and organization people like Tomsky and Rykov, who for various reasons were committed to a program of caution and slow reform. This opposition, too, was eliminated from positions of influence after a very brief struggle. Acknowledging that economic as well as political stagnation were major dangers facing the Soviet regime, Stalin now launched a program of rapid industrialization on the basis of a five-year plan—the most ambitious, not to say reckless, of the various plans elaborated by the party economists. Stalin himself later referred to the years of this first five-year plan as another revolution (adding that it was a revolution made from above), and rightly so, because not only did the five-year plans achieve revolutionary changes in the economic, social, political, and cultural fabric of Russia but these changes were initiated in truly revolutionary frenzy, which gripped the party and imparted its spirit to all fields of endeavor.

The plan for industrialization was carried out with utter disregard for considerations of economic balance or rationality, or for the demands of the consumer. Instead, it was executed as a desperate crash program. The Russian population again suffered lean years, with a drastic lowering of living standards, as every ounce of available energy—human as well as material—was pressed into service and pumped into investment. In agriculture the new revolution brought with it a virtual civil war against the peasantry. The regime wanted to neutralize the peasants once and forever as a potential political force, wanted to subject them to economic, political, and cultural controls and pressures, and particularly wished to make sure that every year's harvest would reach the hungry mouths of the city dwellers. For without food and agricultural raw materials, the industrialization effort would be doomed. To secure these ends, the party decided to abolish private enterprise in farming and force the peasants into cooperative, or collective, farms, where they would be subject to all these controls, primarily because collective farms would not own the essential means of production—tractors and implements—but would have to rent them from government pools. Motor and repair shops were therefore in a position of control and could become centers not only for the economic exploitation of the farmers but also for their political control and education and for efforts to urbanize the farm population.

Peasant resistance to the attempt to "collectivize" them was bitter and persistent, and the regime succeeded in overcoming it only through a virtual civil war, in which hundreds of thousands of peasants lost their lives, millions were rendered destitute, and the agricultural economy of the Soviet Union suffered damages that were not repaired until more than twenty years later. In the wake of collectivization, a disastrous famine killed millions of Soviet citizens.

For the first few years the industrialization was accompanied by a new radicalism in culture and educational affairs, a new stress on proletarian exclusiveness, but in other aspects of Soviet Russia moved further away from socialist goals and methods. The workers, whose trade unions during the NEP had retained at least a modicum of bargaining and administrative power, were totally subjected to discipline under a new managerial system. Where formerly Russia's government and industry had been managed "collectively," that is, through administrative committees, a command principle was now instituted whereby all agencies were to be run by single managers with full authority and responsibility. The country's administration was thus streamlined to resemble the organization and management of giant corporations in the Western world—a process through which the party itself had already gone some years before.

Two additional developments were required before Soviet Russia was tranformed into the type of society it is today. I shall call one of these the cultural counterrevolution.* The other one is

*The term has been suggested by my friend Robert V. Daniels.

known as the Great Purge. The two phenomena are closely related to each other.

The origins and meaning of the Great Purge remain a matter of conjecture and controversy. The paranoid and vengeful personality of Stalin is as unsatisfactory an explanation as the totalitarian pattern of Soviet rule with its presumed need for an occasional personnel turnover through the means of a bloody housecleaning. We must take into consideration the tremendous difficulties faced by Stalin's regime in the 1930s. The reckless pace of industrialization and collectivization had led to serious bottlenecks and deficiencies in the national economy. In the party, the government, and the economy, serious morale problems were created by the arbitrariness with which impossible tasks were imposed on ill-trained personnel or inadequate facilities. In international affairs the Soviet Union began to face new grave threats from strong neighbors to the west and the east. It is plausible to assume that the victims of the Great Purge served, among other things, as scapegoats on whom all blame for these failures could be heaped. Furthermore, numerous party members may have been in a state of genuine panic and therefore quite receptive to what was alleged to be evidence of sabotage, treason, and the like. Most historians, finally, would point out that the cultural counterrevolution, the thorough bureaucratization of Russia, the decided turn away from revolutionary endeavors, and the entire trend of development in Soviet politics under Stalin's rule could not have been carried out successfully as long as the old Bolsheviks were still alive who had helped make the revolution, who had been raised in a spirit of utopian radicalism and Marxist critique, and who would not have found it possible to adjust to Stalinist society without continually rebelling against it. The revolutionary generation, perhaps, was unfit for life in the society the revolution had created.

Whatever the reasons, the fact is that between 1935 and 1938 the USSR became the stage for a veritable orgy of police activity, in which the party, the government apparatus, the economy, the armed forces, the schools and universities, and all the professions were decimated, especially in their higher ranks, from which vast numbers of personnel disappeared into the labor camps or execution dungeons of the secret police. In the Communist party, nearly everyone who had ever disagreed with the dictator was physically eliminated; the same fate befell countless officials within the party and outside of it who were denounced for, or suspected of, harboring dissent. As a result, the administrative body of Soviet society was decapitated; an entire generation of leaders fell victims to the purge and an entire generation of younger ones moved up to fill their places. Furthermore, it might be said that the purge destroyed the Communist party, although I know of no one who has expressed this fact so drastically. Nonetheless I believe it to be true. Not only did the Great Purge kill off or jail almost all those who had been members of the party before and during the revolution of 1917. In that sense, the party of Lenin certainly was destroyed. But in addition the place and function that the party had had in Soviet society were changed so drastically that we might speak of its destruction. In the first two decades of the Russian Revolution, the party had been the sovereign of the Soviet Union, to use an old-fashioned term. It had been in charge. It had acted as if it owned the country or as if it were administering it in the name of the working class. This undisputed sovereignty of the party was replaced, in the Great Purge, by the undisputed sovereignty of Josef Stalin. He made use of the party as one of the instruments of his rule, but he used it no more, and in practice assigned no greater importance to it than to the government administration or the political police. To be precise, Stalin's central organ of rule was his personal secretariat, which, even though it had close connections with the party and the police, was yet apart from them and above them, assigning them a secondary role.*

The cultural counterrevolution was a process of transformation consummated about the time of the Great Purge. Its outward manifestation was a decided return to traditionalism in education, art, social science, mores, and other elements that make up a society's cultural life. It included such developments as the reintroduction of military ranks and tsarist-style uniforms, the strengthening of the family and of the authority of both parents and teachers, and the abandonment of *avant-garde* art styles in favor of the naive naturalism of what Hitler called "heroic art" and which in the USSR is called "socialist realism."

---

*We might recognize the justification for asserting that the party was destroyed in the following figures of the proportion of voting delegates at party congresses who were party members before 1921, that is, before the end of the civil war:

> Seventeenth Congress (1934) . . . . 80.0 per cent
> Eighteenth Congress (1939) . . . . 19.4 per cent

But if this was a *return* to traditionalism, from where did it return? The answer is, from Marxism. True, Marxism remained as the acknowledged creed of the Soviet state, hailed as the last word in social and natural science as well as philosophy, elevated to the status of official dogma. But only the words of Marx became dogma; essential elements of what he meant and what he wanted were abandoned. In returning to traditionalism in cultural and intellectual life, the Soviet regime rejected at least two major elements of Marxism. One was the dream of a society without alienation or (to eschew utopianism) without that surplus alienation which goes beyond the minimum of alienation required to keep a modern industrial economy operating,* a dream that had been kept very much alive in the period of the NEP and the First Five-Year Plan. The regime that emerged in the mid-1930s seems to have come to the conclusion that the yearning for such a society, for the institutions and processes depicted in Lenin's *The State and Revolution*, would never, or not for a very long time, be satisfied, and that the yearning itself, therefore, was disturbing and disruptive. So it became subversive to talk about or ask for the withering away of the state, the disappearance of oppressive institutions and social or economic inequality. At the same time, Marxist doctrines or words were twisted in such a fashion as to create the impression that a major portion of the dreams of Marx and Engels had indeed come true. Socialism had been achieved. The class struggle had been abolished. The Soviet people were a happy people.

The assertion that socialism had been achieved implied the rejection of one other element of Marxism, namely, the use of social science for the purpose of analyzing social phenomena as the superstructure of exploitative economic systems. Marxism had not been only a dream of the future. It had also been critical of the past and the present; it is by its very method and orientation a critical social theory. Soviet society, however, continued to incorporate intense alienation of all its citizens, which the Soviet Union became altogether unwilling to admit. Soviet theory has been reluctant to concede that its own society incorporates repression, domination, and exploitation. At most, it hints at remaining differences between the interests of the state and those of the individual. Being unwilling to admit these repressive

*The term "surplus alienation" is adapted from Herbert Marcuse, *Eros and Civilization* (Boston, 1956).

features, it cannot, of course, justify them, as well it might be able
to do. As a matter of fact, we might say that one of the main
distinguishing features of Stalinist theory is this unwillingness to
admit the necessity (in Bolshevik terms) for repressive measures.
Stalin and his comrades obviously did not dare take the people
into their confidence about the hard road that lay ahead in the
drive for rapid industrialization. I think that here lies the main
difference between Stalin and Trotsky: The policies they advocated were similar, but the latter was honest about their harsh-
ness, whereas Stalinism sought to conceal it behind phrases to
the effect that the Soviet world is the best of all possible worlds.
Important among the ideological taboos resulting from this unwillingness to look reality in the face is the inability to admit that
the isolation of the "proletarian" revolution in a backward peasant country was, from the point of view of original Marxism, a
historical freak and, from the point of view of the proletarian
world revolution, an unmitigated disaster. There was therefore
even a marked reluctance to admit that tsarist Russia was a
backward society in comparison with Western Europe. These
ideological taboos have little to do with Marxism; on the contrary,
they are in sharp contradiction to it. Marxist theory, in fact, has
been thoroughly emasculated and converted into apologetics.
Under Stalin, even though Marx and Engels were the prophets of
Soviet society, their writings were availabe to Soviet readers only
in expurgated editions; their earlier works particularly were
either suppressed or explained away, for these works contain in
the clearest form their critique of domination and their yearning
for liberty. Entire concepts were eliminated from the storehouse
of Marxist methods, because they might yield conclusions un-
comfortable to the regime. Occasionally, Stalin even ventured to
criticize some of their works openly; for instance, he denounced
Engels for his hatred of tsarist Russia and his eagerness to see
Western Europe united in a war to destroy that hated state.

The turn to traditionalism came to pervade all of Soviet
culture. In the teaching of history, the preoccupation with class
wars and economic developments and with the depressing
features of tsarist Russia's past gave way to the old-fashioned
kings-and-battles approach familiar to us from our own high
school texts; and the heroes no longer were the exploited masses
but Russian emperors, generals, and conquerors of backward people

in the Caucasus and Central Asia. Art turned into a weapon of mass propaganda, using the vehicle of popular style and expressing ideas designed to give cheer to the laboring masses. The idea of equality, which had inspired many of the deeds of the Revolution and the civil war, now was denounced as a petit-bourgeois delusion; henceforth in thought and in fact Soviet society came to lay stress on social differences, for the avowed purpose of providing incentives that had previously been considered unnecessary. By emphasizing differences of salary and rank, peak performance was encouraged, so that the Soviet population came under the sway of what Marcuse has called the "performance principle." To back up the system of rewards, police terror and concentration camps were provided, imposing stern sanctions on anyone not conforming to the regime's demands. Finally, as discussed, a social theory was carefully designed not to unmask inequalities and alienation but to conceal them. Malfunctions, henceforth, were explained not as the symptoms of an ill social system (as Marx and Engels would have done) but as moral failings of individuals who were either weak and therefore had to be treated sternly or who were criminal conspirators who had to be eliminated. In all these and many other fields, Soviet culture returned to the Victorian age.

With these developments, Soviet life was set for the next two decades. In short, out of the purges, the first two five-year plans, the collectivization campaign, and the cultural counterrevolution, Stalinist society emerged. Soviet society acquired a certain stability for the first time. Henceforth, it might still undergo changes, but they would be less drastic in scope and less violent in form.

CHAPTER 6

The System That Stalin Built

Stalin continued to rule the Union of Soviet Socialist Republics until his death in March 1953. The most spectacular event of his long reign probably was the country's involvement in World War II. From this war, after initial military disasters, the Soviet Union emerged victorious, although gravely damaged: Millions of lives were lost, untold material wealth destroyed. The purpose of this chapter is not, however, to dwell on the events of the war but on the nature of the system Stalin built and the ideology by which he sought to justify it.

It might be useful to begin by recognizing the Soviet Union as a relatively underdeveloped country engaged in a crash program to exploit its resources and outstrip the Western world in productivity and economic potential. It comprises a population of many languages, races, religions, and cultures that sixty years ago consisted primarily of rural people, peasants or nomads, on a level of technology, literacy, and productivity below that of urban and industrial Europe and North America. These were people without a strong tradition of self-government, yet they were rebellious against their ruling elites. More than fifty years ago the Communist party ruling over these people decided to make an all-out effort to industrialize their country as rapidly as possible. Whether this was a decision that sooner or later had to be taken, regardless of who was in power or what motives were guides, is a highly controversial question and must be left unanswered here. In any event, the decision was taken.

To carry it out, the Soviet social system had to undergo a number of adjustments, and the party had to take certain broad measures. Industrialization of an undeveloped economy requires, first of all, the marshaling of all material and human resources, hence an austerity regime in which every available scrap of energy is expended for the construction effort and every ounce of material resource that can be diverted from consumption is invested. Rapid industrialization, in other words, calls for continued low living standards and forbids consumer sovereignty. This applies all the more to a revolutionary regime surrounded by hostile neighbors, who cannot be expected to help the industrialization effort by large-scale material and technical assistance or long-term credits. The Soviet Union was forced to pull itself out of the morass of underdevelopment by its own bootstraps. From all this it becomes clear that, second, industrialization under such circumstances can be accomplished only through central organization and strict discipline, including a managed system of rewards and sanctions. While centralized planning and organized inequality are not necessarily incompatible with political liberty and representative democracy, it is nonetheless obvious that the planners and managers themselves are likely to look at constitutional democracy as a luxury that a country in the process of rapid industrialization cannot afford. And if we look at the ruthlessness of the Soviet regime and at the starkness of the material austerity it imposed on its population, we have to conclude that such measures could have been carried out only by a powerful dictatorship ruling against the will of the people.

Forced saving and political dictatorship alone, however, are not sufficient. One more measure is required to achieve industrialization; that is the training of the population for life in the machine age. Americans ought to be familiar with the adjustments this transformation in the way of life requires, with the difficulty of shedding traditions, beliefs, and behavior patterns that have become dysfunctional in the machine age. We know the pains of adjustment in the style of life that are being suffered as America transforms itself from a country of farmers and petty merchants into a modern industrial and corporate giant. These pains of acculturation are intensified many times when a country like Russia engages in a crash program of industrialization. They are intensified because Soviet Russia has attempted to do in one generation what America has been doing for the last two hundred years and because the cultural level from which most of Russia started was even more remote from the way of life of the atomic age than was the society of Jefferson or Jackson. Lenin, for one, was aware of the magnitude and rapidity of the transformation he wished to bring about and fittingly called it a cultural revolution. In my opinion, this cultural revolution is the most difficult of all the tasks the Russian Communist party has set itself.

POWER STRUCTURE

In describing the social relationships that have grown out of these problems, let us begin by a summary of the power structure in Soviet society. In his book on the process of politics in the United States, David Truman distinguishes between two major types of government existing in the modern world, constitutional government and corporate government. In describing the latter, he was concerned primarily with the manner in which such associations as business corporations and organized interest groups manage their affairs. But I believe we can easily apply his model to the Soviet Union as a whole. Some of its key features include the differentiation between the functions of the owner and the manager; the hierarchic command system of decision making, which must be contrasted to responsible and representative government; the bureaucratic (rather than democratic) division of powers; and the servile and subject status of the lower ranks, for whom final recourse against the commands of the organization lies only outside that organization. One of the principal differences between a Western corporation and the USSR therefore lies in the fact that the aggrieved employee of a Western corporation can quit the organization more readily than a Soviet citizen, who in most cases has no possibility whatsoever of escaping from the society. And short of quitting, the employee can appeal to authorities outside the corporation. Despite this and other major differences, I think it is useful to compare the USSR to a giant corporate enterprise in order to understand some of its structural features.

It is difficult to define the owners of USSR, Incorporated, just as it is difficult to define precisely who owns General Motors. Certainly some own it more than others, or we might say that the quality of ownership varies with the quantity. Ownership of a few shares entitles one to a small share of the profits, whereas ownership of a substantial portfolio carries with it the right to sit on the board of directors, which hires and fires the managers and sets policies for the corporation. If we are right in saying that, for practical purposes, the Communist party might be said to own the Soviet Union, we have to understand that the ownership functions of the rank-and-file party member are not very meaningful. Let me add at once that the Communist party does not have legal title to the USSR and does not claim it. Ownership, however, may be defined not only in legal but also in sociological terms. In the latter case ownership is established as soon as individuals or groups behave *as if they owned* an enterprise. And the Communist party of the Soviet Union, especially its "board of directors," certainly does so behave. It treats the country as if it were its property. To use a traditional term of political science, the party acts as the *sovereign* in the Soviet Union—and, historically as well as philosophically, the concepts of sovereignty and property are virtually synonymous. To be sure, just as in the Western corporation ownership and management functions are tending more and more to be united in the same persons, so in the enterprise USSR, Incorporated, party members and managers (such as government officials) are often the same persons. And yet, a significant number of party members function solely as party administrators. They are the inner core of the party, the *aktiv*, as it is called in the Soviet Union, whose most successful members form the majority of such policy-making directorates as the Central Committee, the Secretariat, and the Politburo. If we speak of the party as the sovereign owner of the USSR, then, it seems we must mean particularly the party *aktiv*, a ruling elite about whose size, composition, and informal structure we have only the sketchiest information. It is also what is meant by the Soviet citizen when he or she talks about "the party."

The party itself is much larger than its active core, for it includes the millions of members who are active professionally in other pursuits and whose party membership is therefore in the nature of additional duty. It is today a *cadre* party, which means that its members are selected from those citizens who occupy positions of respect, responsibility, and authority in all the many professions or pursuits to which Soviet citizens may be devoted. One might be tempted to say that the party recruits those members of Soviet society who in our society would become members of country clubs, although the criterion for selection is not wealth but managerial or technical responsibility. Like membership in a country club, party membership is at times an indispensable help in furthering one's career or even a precondition for various sensitive or responsible assignments. Unlike country club membership, however, it does not promote the pursuit of golf, swimming, dancing, or other diversions. Instead, it tends to become an arduous and onerous additonal duty. Party members are expected to be active in the various party activities, they are supposed to educate themselves further in the history and ideology of the party, and finally, they are assumed to lead exemplary lives as model citizens. Among those who are underrepresented in the party are not only people in the humbler professions, especially peasants, but also women, including professionally active women. The double burden they still face in the Soviet Union as both wage earners and homemakers leaves most of them little time to be sufficiently active in the party.

As the sovereign owner of Soviet society, the party (in its highest organizations) not only makes the basic decisions of public policy; on all its levels of organization it also sees to it that these decisions are carried out. It concerns itself, furthermore, with the selection and assignment of the top managers in all fields of endeavor and, finally, strives to propagate its views among the population. We might compare the individual party member to the information and education officer in our armed forces, who is supposed to inform others about current world affairs to tell them "what they are fighting for" or "whom they are fighting against." In addition, the party acts as the cheerleader of Soviet society, who through rallies, demonstrations, and publicity of various kinds seeks to build enthusiasm and morale. In everything that is done in Soviet society, the party claims to represent the people, to act in their name and in their behalf and for their benefit. Such claims cannot, of course, be proven and will be self-evident only to those who are already convinced. Among the population of the Soviet Union, there doubtless are people so convinced and also people who are not. The evidence suggests that various members of Soviet society admire the party, or tolerate it as a necessary evil, or hate it with all their heart. The gulf between the party and the people seems to be deepest in rural areas and among the national minorities. In the countryside the Communist party at times appears like an army of occupation or a militant church *in partibus infidelium*, while in Central Asia, Buriat-Mongolia, and other minority areas it assumes some of the aspects of a colonial administration (although there are significant differences between the "colonialism" of the Soviet Union and that of Western nations).

The organization of the party is well adapted to its various tasks. Apart from the strong predominance of centralistic tendencies and the absence of any meaningful democratic procedures, the most notable feature is the mixture of territorial with functional principles of organization. On the higher levels the party is subdivided into regional, provincial, local, and similar territorial organizations, all of which, together with the all-Union headquarters in Moscow, have usually had staff organizations dealing with the functional divisions of Soviet life and activities—the economy, the armed forces, education, art, youth activities, national minorities, and the like. At the grass-roots level, however, the territorial principle is abandoned for the functional one: With few exceptions, the party primary organizations (which have evolved from the conspiratorial cells of prerevolutionary days) are formed within economic or administrative organizations, such as workshops, farms, scientific institutes, army units, or government offices. The party unit thus formed takes charge, as it were, of the organization, regards it as "its own," and functions as a representative of the sovereign. The party primary organization is composed only of members of the parent body—a committee of it, in a sense—and it does act as some sort of steering committee. But, even though formed only of men and women who work in the organization, it is in reality the *direct* representative of the entire party.

I deliberately stress the word *direct*. For after all, the ministry, or the regional planning and executive organization, and also the bank, the public attorney, and other supervisory or command organizations including the political police, all represent the party, however indirectly. All nonparty organizations in the USSR are, in effect, departments or divisions of the overall enterprise, USSR, Incorporated. This is expressed most clearly in the fact that appointments to positions of authority in any one of the organizations and associations of Soviet society are subject to party supervision through an institution or practice called *nomenklatura*. The *nomenklatura* of any organization simply is that list of positions which cannot be filled without the advice and consent of the party; and in every case it also specifies precisely which party organization is to be brought into the appointment process. In addition, any Soviet organization—economic, administrative, cultural, military, or whatever—is subjected to the party through numerous command or supervisory channels at one and the same time. Soviet society can therefore be seen as an administrative maze of parallel hierarchies. We may speak of the trinity of party, government, and police as the main pillars of this structure, or looking at the economic enterprise, we may see that trinity dissolve into a multiplicity of legal, financial, economic, political, and police hierarchies, which may be working in harmony or may be vying with each other for control or jurisdiction. Whether separately or jointly, however, they all impose their particular tasks on the managers and lower personnel of the given unit.

Chief among the party's agencies in managing the country is the government, which includes not only most of the legislative, administrative, judicial, military, and penal institutions that are part of all modern governments, but also the entire economy, all educational and scientific pursuits, health services, and even entertainment and cultural endeavors. Certain processes of this government can be studied more easily than others and are therefore better known. Not known at all among Western students of the Soviet way of life is the legislative process. The constitution notwithstanding, policy decisions taking the form of laws, regulations, or decrees are discussed, formulated, and adopted behind closed doors, and we have only the scantiest information even concerning who discusses them, what the procedures are, and so forth. It is clear, however, that the major task that the enterprise USSR, Incorporated, has set itself is the task of production, or better, of rapid economic growth. In Soviet rhetoric, the task is defined as one of catching up with, and outstripping, the United States in production and productivity.

The major political decisions for the managers of the enterprise during any one period are therefore the production plan and its supplementary decisions. Supplementary directives include financial plans, raw materials utilization plans, labor plans, and others. The shaping of all these and the major production plans is a complex and continual operation based on information regarding available resources and skills, on experience regarding past performance, and on the political decision regarding priorities in production. The execution of the plan is the responsibility of the Council of Ministers, but in accordance with the principle of individual managerial responsibility, the Soviet enterprise is given a certain degree of autonomy. It is set up to resemble a business firm, with its own capital and cash resources. It deals with other enterprises of the Soviet economy through the means of contracts; there is a system of laws governing contractual relationships and a court system to enforce them. Restricted as his or her discretion is, the director of a Soviet firm is responsible not only for adherence to the various plans, laws, and directives specifying permissible ranges of the use of materials, labor, credit, and the like but is also responsible for supposedly operating at a profit; most of all, the firm is expected to meet or outstrip the production goals handed down from the planning authorities. Under such multiple pressures, with high rewards offered for outstanding performance and severe sanctions imposed for a poor showing, Soviet production managers have become part of a rat race very similar to that of their American colleagues. Similar conditions, moreover, are imposed on responsible personnel in noneconomic fields—physicians, artists, teachers, scholars, administrators, and even members of the working class itself. The rat race is as all-pervasive in Soviet society as it is in America.

In the Soviet Union, it is caused by a coincidence of various factors. First, the party asks all citizens to work their very hardest and give their very best. The rule of this performance principle, as Marcuse calls it, is enforced not only by pitting fellow citizens and rival organizations against each other in managed competition but also by manipulating rewards in such a fashion that only peak performance is rewarded adequately. Second, the rat race is a function of the multiplicity of authorities imposing often conflicting standards of behavior on the administrator. Whatever a Soviet manager does, he or she is often forced to violate some standards in order to satisfy others because, taken together, all the commands are impossible to carry out. While at first glance the result is inefficiency and chaos, this approach may nonetheless be a very satisfactory and efficient method of management for the party. Through its many agencies, the party enforces its standards selectively and therefore wields a complex administrative machinery that is very sensitive to subtle changes in policy. Such changes need not be announced formally but can be signaled by a slight shift in the selective enforcement of multiple standards. The party enjoys not only the possibility of manipulating the society but also the privilege of not having to contradict itself, while the lower managerial personnel take all the risk. They are struck with sanctions when shifts occur.*

The development of Soviet Russia into a modern industrial society has brought with it tendencies of unmeasurable strength toward the differentiation of special groups within the power elite, tendencies similar to those characterizing Western societies. Such groups, to which we can attribute different and conflicting interests, are based on loyalty to leaders, commitment to diverging policies, fields of professional specialization, or identification with particular regions or localities. In the concrete, these various interests doubtless overlap and conflict with each other, any one individual being a member of many identifiable groups. Without doubt, also, the resulting tendencies toward the development of some sort of pluralism are held in check by the strong bonds of joint interests which all members of the Soviet power elite have in common when they face the outside world and their own population. Moreover, some of the tendencies toward pluralism were checked when, after Stalin's death, the party resumed that sovereign position in Soviet society which it might be said to have lost between 1938 and 1953.

TYPES OF SOCIAL CONTROL

It used to be fashionable to describe the USSR as a *totalitarian* society. The word came into vogue in the Western world after World War II, when the unspeakable inhumanities of the Nazi

---

*An interesting theory incorporating the selective enforcement of conflicting standards in Soviet administration is developed by Andrew Gunder Frank, "The Organization of Economic Activity in the Soviet Union," *Weltwirtschaftliches Archiv*, Vol. 78, No. 1 (1957), pp. 104–156.

regime became a matter of public record. The term carries with it the notion of a regime's utter disregard of the dignity, feelings, and interests of its citizens. It reeks of the arbitrary and bloody police state, evokes nocturnal arrests and the concentration camp. Since then, some not very successful attempts have been made to refine the concept and to portray totalitarianism as a unique phenomenon of our century. When I use the term, I am thinking primarily of a society that attempts to control its citizens totally, a regime in which not the slightest degree of autonomy is conceded to individuals or groups, whatever their endeavor may be, a government which regards every human activity or pursuit as a matter of public policy. In this sense, the Soviet Union comes closer to the totalitarian model than any other modern society, although, with due allowance for technological differences, it can be argued that many societies of the past were governed according to similar totalitarian principles and manifested most if not all the essential traits of the totalitarian syndrome.

Totalitarianism, if indeed it can be described so that social scientists would agree on the definition, probably is the political framework of the crash-program phase of communist development. If this is acceptable, how then should one characterize the Soviet and other communist systems after the threshold of industrialization has been crossed, the system settles down into a comparatively stable mold, and the methods and instruments of totalitarian rule are, by and large, dismantled?

My answer would be that in the crash program phase, and even more so afterwards, communist societies in their structure and functioning closely resemble those large, complex administrative organizations which we call bureaucracies. Public life in the Soviet Union, in Eastern Europe, and also in the People's Republic of China generally goes on within a framework of formal institutions, informal groupings, and processes that strikingly resemble those of large bureaucracies in other parts of the world. Hence communist societies share with modern bureaucracies the managerial problems and irrationalities; the various modes of individual adjustment to these problems tend to be similar, and the personality types arising in them are apt to be alike. In short, communist societies can be defined as modern bureaucracies writ large—that is, societies in which the managerial forms and patterns characterizing business corporations, public institutions, army posts and battleships, large governmental agencies, and the like are extended to the management of the entire society.

The totalitarian and the bureaucratic models of Stalinist and post-Stalinist society may well be complementary rather than mutually exclusive. Most scholars would agree that there is little if anything in the lives and activities of Soviet citizens that the party does not regard as a matter of public policy and seek to manage or control—political activities, economic and professional performance, education and employment; both the production and enjoyment of entertainment, art, and all leisure activities; family life, ideas and beliefs, and even emotions, or at least their outward manifestations. In the eyes of many students, therefore, the Soviet system of government is characterized primarily by the universal urge to *control*, which they tend to derive from an insatiable urge to dominate. In their writings, the attempt to establish total control at times becomes the very essence of the Soviet way of life, subsuming all other motives and relationships; communist theory, too, is reduced to an organizational scheme designed to establish universal controls.*

Such a one-sided theory must be supplemented by additional explanations. A partial explanation lies in the fact that the economic goals of Soviet society (as defined by its power elite, to be sure) require a good deal of centralized planning and control. The relationship between economic goals and political systems, once the prime interest of students in political economy, has not in recent times received the attention it deserves. But it does seem clear that economic systems can be classified according to the goals to which they give priority, such as economic growth, equitable distribution (welfare state), the preservation of property rights, the most rational allocation of resources, and perhaps others. If it is true that to every one of these goals a specific political structure is best suited, then undoubtedly centralization rather than decentralization, command rather than democracy, austerity rather than consumer sovereignty, seem to be designed to achieve rapid economic growth, and there are scholars who ex-

*Merle Fainsod, *How Russia Is Ruled* (Cambridge, Mass., 1953), sees the Soviet political system almost entirely as an instrument of control, neglecting the many other functions performed by its governmental institutions and processes. For a view of the Soviet system as the purest specimen of a new species of government, called totalitarianism, see Bertram D. Wolfe, *Communist Totalitarianism* (Boston, 1961).

pect that the attainment of this goal would open the way for a certain mellowing of the Soviet political system. Such a process of mellowing need not imply the certain emergence of constitutional government of either the Anglo-Saxon or the French type. Although even such a development should not, perhaps, be dismissed as entirely impossible, it seems far more likely, at this time, to assume that Soviet society will increasingly be characterized by a complex, pluralistic structure of interlocking bureaucratic hierarchies, perpetually straining under conflicting centralist and centrifugal tendencies, a unity containing ever-increasing diversity. Again, in visualizing these trends of development, the model I have in mind is that of the giant Western corporation.

I should like to point out again in this connection that economic growth, or more precisely, the rapid industrialization of a "backward" country, requires not only heavy capital investment and hence consumer austerity, which has to be forced on people, not only centralized management, planning, and control of the economic machinery, not only hard work from every citizen, from each according to his or her ability; it also requires that cultural revolution which Lenin demanded as early as 1922. And it is my belief that the exigencies of this concerted effort to transform a vast nation's entire way of life are as much responsible for Soviet totalitarianism as any other factor we have named. To be sure, Lenin said that the Soviet government must attempt to "build socialism" with the human material it found available in Russia. In fact, however, once the program of industrialization was started in earnest, the party tried to create the "new Soviet human being," an individual well fitted to help in the effort to build and run a modern industrial establishment, an individual equipped to live according to the rhythm of the machine rather than the rhythm of nature.

The methods used by the Soviet regime to control its population for these ends can be grouped in four main categories: rewards, sanctions, education, and organization.

Rewards. Chief among the rewards is organized inequality, according to the motto, "To each according to his work." In the USSR, the entire society is, as it were, earning piece-rate wages, sharply graded, with regressive taxation accenting the differences. Soviet society has been made rank conscious, for the rewards for top performance include deference made visible by uniforms, badges, titles, and similar tokens of status.

Moreover, the Soviet Union must now be considered a consumer society, that is, a society in which working to make one's private life, one's home, and one's family's existence more comfortable and affluent is officially recognized as a worthy endeavor. In the early decades of the Russian Revolution the exemplary Soviet citizen or party hero was supposed to be proud of asceticism, of the ability to endure material hardship and deprivation. Today that citizen is more likely to be portrayed as someone who is proud to have succeeded, to have attained elite status and high responsibility as well as the material and status benefits that come with it. Although the industrial working class is still declared to be the most creative and productive element in society and to be proud of this, working-class parents are also supposed to be proud when their children have managed to rise to higher white-collar positions. In short, the USSR has become a stratified society, with notable differences in affluence, life styles, and prestige; significant numbers of people live below the officially defined poverty line while the life style of the top elite resembles that of the wealthy class in capitalist societies. The resultant possibilities for upward social mobility cannot but act as a spur to career-minded citizens.

Equally important as rewards for cooperation are the material benefits granted to all citizens regardless of performance. The USSR is a welfare state, in the sense that it strives to eliminate the most grievous hardships caused by disaster, disease, and old age and tries to raise the material level of living for all. The regime has at last begun to convince many of its citizens that the collective effort will result in material benefits for each individual, that unselfish work for little reward may therefore be no more than the rational pursuit of each individual's self-interest. Evidence of graft and high living among the power elite contradict this theory, but a majority of the population may nonetheless have accepted it. The steady improvement in the living standards, especially the improvement in social services such as education, medical help, and old-age security, have acted as powerful arguments in this direction. So also have the indications (of which most Soviet citizens are aware) that at last the USSR is showing itself capable of catching up with the West in industrial production and scientific achievement. The Soviet citizen is beginning to feel like a partner, albeit a lowly one, in a growing and successful enterprise. At the same time, the world-wide depression of the 1980s has had its impact on the Soviet economy as well. The once-spectacular rise in production has leveled off, Soviet agriculture seems to be in recurrent crisis, and numerous other difficulties have resulted in grave inefficiencies. Life for average Soviet citizens still is hard, and the regime does not have the resources to meet their rising expectations.

I have suggested that opportunities for upward social mobility were part of the reward package the Soviet system offered its citizens. For several decades the USSR was expanding, and the demand for talented and skilled personnel in every field seemed insatiable. It appeared to be a society with plenty of room at the top—not the very top perhaps, but certainly in the top layer of experts and managers. It seemed to be a society wide open for young people of promise who were willing to work hard. But here also, it may well be that a point of satiation or near-satiation has been reached, which may make it more and more difficult to fulfill rising expectations in this area.

Sanctions. Societies and cultures have not only different hierarchies of values but also different conceptions of the seriousness of deviant behavior. In modern societies these conceptions are expressed by criminal law. Criminal law in the Soviet Union is designed to inflict harsh punishment on those citizens who refuse to contribute to the social construction effort in the prescribed manner.

Conformity to party standards is enforced, furthermore, by the extralegal terror of the political police. The aim of organized terror in the Soviet system is not so much to punish malperformance as to *prevent* heresy, dissent, or actions hostile to the regime. This is accomplished by keeping a continual check on all citizens' activities, associations, and environmental influences and by punishing those individuals or groups who on the bases of these influences can be expected to have open or latent tendencies toward disloyalty. Jerzy Gliksman has called this function of the terror "prophylactic justice." But even though this appears to be a very apt description of one of the tasks performed by the political police, it neglects another equally important one, which is that of serving as the eyes and ears of the regime in continually gauging the moods of the population. The secret police, in other words, functions as a public-opinion polling institution and in this fashion also helps to maintain controls. An incidental result of "prophylactic justice" was the use of prison labor on a very large scale in work projects for which, because of their difficulty or hazards or inhuman living conditions, it would have been hard to find volunteers. This notorious labor camp system has been important in Soviet society since the 1920s; the Western world has become thoroughly familiar with its history and its functioning by the work of Aleksandr Solzhenitsyn, especially his *Gulag Archipelago*. The extent to which the use of this method of terror has declined or has been replaced by other forms of control over behavior and thought is controversial, but there seem to be at least some people in high places in Soviet society who doubt the effectiveness of massive punitive measures. Since Stalin's death, his successors have experimented with other means of control, ranging from confinement of dissenters in insane asylums to sanctions wielded by peer groups of colleagues or neighbors, who are empowered to mete out summary punishment to persons unwilling to conform to Soviet standards of work or behavior.

Even if there were no terror whatever, the fact that the Soviet state is virtually the sole employer and educator makes all citizens highly dependent on the authorities and doubtless acts as an effective sanction against deviant behavior. The effectiveness of this hold on the citizens might increase if and when the Soviet economy manages to replace human labor with automatic machines and when structural unemployment replaces perpetual full employment.

Education. Education in the USSR is entirely in the hands of the government; it is both a means of inculcating Soviet values and the party outlook in the younger generation and a method of structuring the labor supply and screening personnel in all branches of activity. To individual Soviet citizens, the educational system is a valuable social service provided without charge, which gives them an opportunity to move upward in the social scale, if they are not screened out by the selection process. Thus the educational system metes out rewards as well as disappointment. It promotes some and keeps others down—*down* meaning in the ranks of workers and collective farmers or in professions that do not carry high prestige, authority, or material rewards.

Education is not confined to schools and universities. In the Soviet Union, as everywhere else, the media of mass communications—the press, radio, television—also function as educational institutions. Moreover, in the USSR, the entertainment media, too, have been made vehicles of the party's educational effort, and so have all other forms of communication, even literature and art, which are promoted and tolerated only as long as they carry the party's message to the masses. Whatever they may hear, see, or read, Soviet citizens are thus likely to receive messages sent by the party with the aim of making them more loyal and cooperative, more "conscious," citizens. In short, all communications media in Soviet society serve the purpose of frantic and relentless indoctrination designed to make all citizens accept fully and genuinely the values and goals of the political leadership. This, on the whole, has been quite successful in socializing citizens.

Organization. Whatever the success of this unending and inescapable educational effort, it could be achieved only because all media of communication, from schools to billboards, from the press to opera houses, are directly or indirectly in the hands of the party. The party ensures the success of its many efforts at indoctrination, control, and management by wielding control over all the organizations within which the individuals carry on their various activities.

In modern industrial societies everywhere, fewer and fewer functions are carried out by the isolated individual. Instead, the functions of society are performed by organizations and associations, both formal and informal. One founder of Russian communism, Lenin, realized the political implications of this fact. He realized that an elite could dominate the many organizations within which men and women play their social roles. Organizations, said Lenin, are transmission belts transferring to all members the impetus given by the power behind the organization. Organization is the tool by which men and women can be manipulated.

Accordingly, the party in the USSR has attempted to get hold of all organizations and associations, formal and informal, constituting the society. It has done this with so much success that the entire network of organizations and associations in the Soviet Union is a huge and complex system of what we might call party front organizations. The process by which this organizational mastery of society was achieved is akin to the *Gleichschaltung* of German society undertaken by the National Socialists after coming to power. It is essentially a dual operation. The first step is the destruction of all existing organizations and associations that are not agencies of the party, from rival parties through professional associations to youth organizations and stamp collectors' clubs. In the Soviet Union much of this was accomplished in the period of war communism, but the process was not completed until about fifteen years after the revolution. Once it has been accomplished, a new network of organizations can be created by the party, in which all key positions are filled by party members subject to party directives and discipline. The result of this reorganization (which began long before the destruction of the old social structure was completed) will be that many seemingly spontaneous activities are in fact carried out under the planning, supervision, and control of the party. This, far more than nighttime arrests and labor camps, is the essence of Soviet totalitarianism.

Culture. What has held this system together is not only centralized organization, threats of punishment and promises of rewards, and a well-coordinated national system of child-rearing and educational institutions, but also an official ideology, which will be discussed in the next chapter. Even more pervasive than any of these system-maintenance devices, perhaps, is the general spirit of Soviet politics, the most fundamental assumptions about authority, leadership, citizenship, duties, and rights, which form what contemporary social scientists would call the political culture of the Soviet Union. To the outside observer, that culture looks surprisingly similar to what prevailed in the tsarist empire. This observation brings up the question of how much change any revolution, even the most radical one, can effect.

Of course, the Bolshevik revolution produced profound cultural change. It educated a nation of peasants and made them literate; it taught these peasants and their children habits of punctuality and hygiene and a host of skills and practices enabling people to work with machinery and live by the rhythm of the clock. A veritable cultural revolution was instituted by the Leninist regime and carried further under Stalin. In the process of this cultural revolution, the old authorities—tsars, bureaucrats, generals, landlords, and priests—were discredited and removed, but what replaced them often looked surprisingly similar. The similarity is even greater when we look at the reemergence of authority patterns, authority styles, and authority symbols under Stalin. Some scholars looking at the Soviet Union during the last decades of Stalin's rule and observing the deference paid to superiors by their inferiors, the authoritarian tone, the rank-consciousness, the repressive sexual mores, the schoolmaster tone of political indoctrination, and such other indicators argued that the cultural revolution initiated by Lenin ended up in a cultural counterrevolution under Stalin. In one of the following chapters, I shall try to illustrate this point by examining the official self-image of the Soviet Union, that is, Soviet ideology.

CHAPTER 7

The Soviet Union Since Stalin

Communist societies are revolutionary societies. This means that they seek to destroy a preexisting social system and substitute a new one. The destruction begins with the fall of the previously established political order and the ascent to power of the Communist party. The party then attempts to undermine and destroy the social structure and culture patterns associated with the old order and to replace them with an entirely new social and political system. The destructive task is difficult and painful, and it is never quite complete; some vestiges of the previous social order remain. The task of system building is even more difficult and, because this difficulty makes the communist regime insecure and impatient, it resorts to Stalinist methods to speed up the process. After some decades of false starts, general chaos, and much waste of material and human resources, however, the party succeeds in establishing a relatively viable new social order. In doing so it creates, among other things, a new social structure and a new political culture—neatly reversing the relationship between social base and political superstructure which Marx had taken for granted. Marx had assumed that the social order gives rise to a political system, not the other way around. In time, however, the newly created social structure and political culture establish and strengthen themselves and, having done so, begin to be seen by the political leaders as a reality with which they have to reckon and to which they have to adjust. The substructure thus begins to assert a measure of sovereignty. Some process like this began in the USSR a few years after the end of World War II.

World War II strained every fiber of the Soviet social fabric. The population at large, the armed forces, and perhaps even the party were unprepared for the German attack, and there was a good deal of demoralization. In the first few weeks, vast areas of territory and hundreds of thousands of troops were lost to the enemy. In some regions, particularly in the Ukraine and the Northern Caucasus, many greeted the German troops as liberators from the communist yoke, only to be disillusioned cruelly by the unspeakable barbarity of German rule in Russia. As everyone knows, the war ended in the defeat of the Germans. But the Soviet Union bore the major brunt of it, and deep scars remained for many years. Millions of men had been lost, other millions maimed for life; countless villages, towns, and cities were razed; the grand effort toward rapid industrialization must have suffered serious setbacks affecting particularly the standard of living of the population.

During the war the Soviet regime made a concerted effort to gain or maintain the loyalty of the entire population. For this purpose, the party deemphasized specifically communist themes in its propaganda and stressed instead the ideas of patriotism. This war was to be a war for the defense of the native land rather than for the defense of communism. In line with this attempt to appeal to all Soviet people, the party opened its ranks to those who had distinguished themselves in battle; it tacitly tolerated peasant encroachments on collective farm property; it demonstratively made its peace with the Church; and by its alliance with the Western democracies it consciously or unconsciously instilled in many Soviet citizens the hope that after the war Soviet Russia would continue to collaborate with the democratic countries and that a more relaxed and a more prosperous life was in store for them.

To curb these hopes, the party decided, once the war had been won, to return to the sternest methods of economic, political, and ideological reconstruction. The party ranks were purged of many who had recently been admitted. Rigid consumer austerity and work discipline were enforced once more, and all ideas about ideological compromises or about future collaboration with the noncommunist West were driven out of the heads of intellectuals with an iron broom. The ensuing campaign to purify Soviet doctrine and eliminate all deviators is often referred to as the *zhdanov-*

shchina, because Andrei Zhdanov, the head of the Leningrad regional party organization and a member of the Politburo, acted as its chief spokesman and inquisitor. But even after his death his policies were continued. As a matter of fact, the political atmosphere inside the country became even more tense in the late forties and early fifties, as additional deviators or presumed deviators were ferreted out, both in Russia and in the countries of Eastern Europe. By 1952 it appeared very much as if another major purge was being prepared in the highest levels of the party, a purge that would engulf Soviet society in a new reign of acute terror. Before these obvious preparations could bear fruit, however, the dictator of the country, Josef Stalin, died, in March 1953.

For years before Stalin's death, scholars in the West had predicted that his passing would lead to an intense struggle for power among his chief lieutenants; and the identity of the one most likely to succeed him had become a matter of widespread speculation. Stalin himself had sought to settle this matter by singling out one of his lieutenants, G. M. Malenkov, as his designated successor. But dictators no longer control things once they are dead and buried; and the top leaders of the party quickly proceeded to make arrangements of their own. Indeed, what ensued was not so much a struggle for power as it was a struggle *against* power, that is, an attempt on the part of the survivors to make sure that another Stalin would not rise up and take over. They wanted the style and substance of Stalin's leadership to be replaced with something different. Malenkov was subtly but surely maneuvered out of the leading position; an attempt made by L. P. Beria, the chief of the entire secret police apparatus, to secure power for himself and his entourage was nipped in the bud; he and his co-conspirators were executed in December 1953. The Soviet Union was going to be ruled by a committee of party leaders, the world was told; and for a few years this arrangement seemed to be working.

Yet every modern society needs to designate a person as the one in charge, the one at whose desk the buck stops; and this need probably is particularly great in societies such as the Soviet Union in which centralized command is a long tradition. Whatever the reasons, within a few years after Stalin's death, Nikita Sergeevich Khrushchev had emerged as the new top leader of the Soviet Union. A man of working-class background who had shown administrative skill, energy, and considerable courage in a wide variety of party assignments, he appeared, in dress and language and behavior, to be a man of the people—accessible, egalitarian, simple, and in many respects very different from the aloof Stalin. His style of management was informal, innovative, impulsive, and at times, bold. At the Twentieth Congress of the Party, in 1956, he surprised the world by making a speech of many hours duration in which he subjected Stalin, and by implication his regime, to guarded but nonetheless merciless criticism, in an obvious attempt to dissociate himself from the dead leader. He made various attempts to revitalize the Soviet economic growth, particularly in agriculture, by encouraging the development of chemical industry, by introducing crops which had proved successful in the United States, and by bold schemes for the reorganization of the party and of the system of economic management.

Khrushchev also sought to re-awaken the party's consciousness about the ultimate aim of the Russian Revolution—the establishment of a utopian society. Around 1960 he announced that within the next twenty years the Soviet Union would in fact reach that utopia. In the following three or four years Soviet ideologists, philosophers, journalists, social scientists, and the like produced a veritable flood of literature spelling out their ideas about what full communism would look like, and by what steps and measures that happy stage would be reached. Communism, according to this image, would be a society in which a life of reasonable comfort could be assured to all citizens, in which all citizens would participate much more than before in public life, so that much of the direction now provided by the center could become superfluous. At the same time, these projections made clear that the communist party would continue to exist as a guide and educator. The state might wither away, but the party would stay.

Khrushchev also made innovations in Soviet foreign policy. He traveled abroad a good deal and was the first Soviet dictator ever to visit the United States. He initiated the sudden break of relations between the USSR and the People's Republic of China; he re-established friendly relations with the communist regime of Yugoslavia, which Stalin had tried to destroy. At the time of the first major unrest in Poland, in 1956, he threatened to intervene with Soviet troops, but withdrew, probably wisely, at the insistence of his Polish colleagues. And in the early 1960s he sought to install Soviet missiles on the island of Cuba, but when confronted by President Kennedy with the threat of nuclear war, he withdrew from the confrontation and dismantled the missile bases—a retreat which probably cost him his career.

Twice his former peers in the party leadership tried to unseat him. The first time it was a coalition of conservatives, led by Stalin's old faithful lieutenant, V. M. Molotov, who were alarmed by his radical departures from Stalin's policies and voted to oust him from office. But while the party's Politburo voted for this motion, the Central Committee, hastily called together for an extraordinary meeting, voted against it; and Khrushchev ousted those who had tried to oust him. The second conspiracy against him succeeded. Frightened by his bold plans for reorganizing the party and the government, which would have endangered many top bureaucrats, these top administrators got together and decided to send Khrushchev into retirement. In his place they eventually installed one of Khrushchev's closest collaborators, L. I. Brezhnev.

Brezhnev quickly reversed many of his predecessor's policies and ruled in very different style; he was conservative and cautious, careful not to upset the bureaucratic order over which he presided. During the fifteen years of his rule the top leadership of the party underwent hardly any changes. The same men who had installed him in office still sat in the Politburo when he died; most of them now were in their seventies and eighties. Under Brezhnev the USSR had become a gerontocracy. These old men ruled the Soviet Union with initial success. In the first period of Brezhnev's rule production figures and living standards in the USSR rose significantly, and the country's stature as a military superpower became more and more obvious. There was an increase in commercial interaction with the Western world, with a corresponding intensification of technology transfers. To be sure, Khrushchev's dreams about reaching the communist utopia by 1980 were scrapped, but now the party began to characterize the system prevailing in the USSR as Developed Socialism, a term which suggested pride in what had been achieved and confidence that the country could now advance toward ever greater success gradually, and without any drastic changes in policy or organization.

Thirty years have passed since Stalin's death. They have been important years for the Soviet Union. The regime has shown the world that it can manage the transition of power from one leader to another in a much less bloody fashion than most observers had expected. For many years its economy continued to grow at a very respectable rate, although most recently this growth rate has leveled off. In many ways the country has been modernized, though at an uneven rate. Even a short stay in any major Soviet city will show to the casual visitor the visible signs of this modernization and the evidence of lag in this process. As a military power, the USSR since Stalin also attained status in a number of fields of scientific exploration. As a superpower, the Soviet Union has widened the scope of its interaction with other nations throughout the world: It now has allies in Asia, Africa, and the Americas, and its navy floats in all the world's oceans.

The educational level of the population has risen. Social services, including medical care, housing, and old-age pensions, have improved. To many observers the development of the Soviet Union since Stalin's death reads like a success story, and the average Soviet citizen, if asked whether he or she was better off today than a generation ago would undoubtedly say yes. At the same time, the curve of economic growth has flattened out in recent years. Improvements in living standards and social services have not kept up with rising expectations, and indeed there is evidence that in some areas the quality of life has declined. All this points to a large number of problem areas in the management of the Soviet Union. A brief overview will show that they range over a wide spectrum of concerns.

One of these problems is that of making wise choices in allocating the country's resources. The famous choice between guns and butter, between rubles spent for military readiness and those spent for consumer satisfaction, is a very real problem, and in the USSR it is complicated by the fact that it is not really that simple a choice. Long-term investment in agriculture and industry would be a third alternative; a fourth would be money spent for foreign commitments. There are many areas of production where equipment and methods are obsolete, but improvement would require heavy investment in new machinery and in the retraining of personnel. To improve output of agricultural produce, some Soviet planners are suggesting expensive irrigation schemes or heavy investment in industries producing farm machinery or fertilizer. In short, a modern economy is compelled to modernize repeatedly in order to remain competitive and viable.

Permanent modernization is not only highly expensive but it also disrupts society. It requires continual retraining of people to teach them new skills and techniques, and it may require new patterns of management and organization. One of the acid tests for the Soviet Union in the coming years may well be whether the system is flexible enough to make these necessary changes and to make them smoothly. The organization and the style of management that Stalin created, and that he left to his successors, were geared specifically to a crash program of industrialization. Stalin was a system builder, the creator of a vast industrial empire. In order to build this empire, he got rid of the people who, together with him, had made the revolution. People who have trained themselves to be revolutionaries. (i.e., system destroyers) are usually not very good at building a new state. System builders in turn may not be very well suited to carry out the tasks required once the system has been erected—the task of system-management. At the same time, it might be argued that those are precisely the kind of people who have come to govern the Soviet Union since Stalin: managers. In the first decades of its existence, the leadership of the USSR was heroic leadership. Lenin and Stalin were men who had the talent and the ruthlessness to mobilize or terrorize millions of people to muster the superhuman efforts necessary to overcome incredibly difficult circumstances. This was done for the purpose of emerging victorious in revolution and war, and of transforming a backward peasant society into a modern superpower. Their successors have risen to prominence out of service to the party and the state. If Lenin and Stalin exercised heroic leadership, their successors were bureaucratic chiefs, installed by their peers because they had demonstrated their competence as administrators and their skill in bureaucratic politics.

However, those skills may not be what is required to solve the problems facing the Soviet state today. When Leonid Il'ich Brezhnev died in November 1982, he left behind him a group of old men whose political habits and views were formed in the Stalin era, who had governed the Soviet Union in highly conservative fashion, shying away from bold reforms of any kind, seemingly abhorring any change. This ruling bureaucracy was internally divided; it appears to be cut off from the people at the grass roots, and harbors a great deal of corruption. There are many grounds for the argument that this system of government is not likely to produce enough vision or courage to make the changes necessary to revitalize the Soviet economy or the spirit of citizenship among the people. Within the next ten years, however, not only Leonid Il'ich Brezhnev but every single member of his 1982 leadership group is likely to be either dead or retired. An entire generation of leaders trained under Stalin will be gone, and that will give the "succession problem" an added dimension, for the next generation of leaders may include people who are far more ready to make bold changes in the organization and management of the system. Meanwhile, it will be interesting to observe what kinds of people will be promoted to fill the growing number of vacancies in the party's Central Committee and in the Politburo.

Whoever may govern the Soviet Union in the last two decades of this century will face not only painful choices in the allocation of scarce resources but other problems as well. The question of whether the system of alliances with other socialist states, especially those of Eastern Europe, is an asset or a liability must have suggested itself to the men in the Kremlin, especially in light of the repeated failure of any communist regime to govern Poland effectively. Poland not only demonstrates the risks and costs of maintaining an empire, it also brings home to the Soviet leadership that discontent and dissatisfaction in the working class demands careful attention lest it explode into serious trouble. There is evidence of deep resentment among the industrial workers of the Soviet Union over their treatment by management and their place within the Soviet pyramid of rewards, status, and deference.

Many observers believe that restiveness and lingering dissatisfaction pervade much of Soviet society. As evidence they would cite the increase in crime, delinquency, alcoholism in the cities, and various other manifestations of alienation. They would also point at the corruption in high places and at the importance of the so-called second economy, a nationwide black market or economic counterculture, as evidence that the official institutions are not functioning as they should.

A very substantial amount of strain inherent in Soviet society is the result of (mostly latent) hostility and resistance shown to the regime by the peasants. On a mass scale, open resistance was offered last at the time of forced collectivization, over fifty years ago. Since then, the peasantry has submitted to the regime most of the time. But it has done so passively and sullenly. It has, despite its submissive attitude, resisted both the party's attempt to press a maximum of agricultural produce from the collective farm system and the effort to educate and urbanize the peasants, wean them away from religious beliefs and make conscious communists of them. The political education and the cultural revolution have not been spectacularly successful in the Soviet countryside. This should not astonish us, for after all, the very meaning of the cultural revolution was to stamp out the peasant way of life. It is the peasants who are least adapted to the machine age and its compelling rhythm, they who are most bound by religion and tradition, and they who more fervently than any other class yearn for private property.

What applies to the peasants applies with even greater emphasis to many of Soviet Russia's national minorities. Not only are most of them overwhelmingly agricultural in their occupation; some of them lived on an even more primitive level of civilization than the Russian peasant, so that the attempt to educate them to communism implies an even more thorough break with their traditional way of life. In addition, the attempt to make the USSR into a homogeneous industrial society necessarily led to the imposition of the Russian language as an all-Soviet *lingua franca* and to the encroachment of Russian personnel and Russian ways on the minority areas. Tendencies toward political independence or autonomy have been stamped out ruthlessly wherever they appeared, and yet by maintaining the federalist form, national self-consciousness has to some extent been kept alive. The memory of past antagonisms and lingering mutual contempt and mutual distrust suggest that national diversity remains a potentially troublesome issue, particularly in light of the demographic trends, which indicate that the Muslim populations of Central Asia might within a few decades become numerically stronger than the Russian or Slavic population.

Every once in a while someone observes that the United States is no longer governable because it has become too big, too complex, too heterogeneous. I am tempted to apply this observation to modern superstates in general. It is not only their bigness and complexity that makes modern superpowers virtually impossible to govern; it is also the perpetual change brought about by continual technological innovation that creates this difficulty. Continual technological innovation brings with it change in the social structure and in processes of management, yet institutions created for the governing of society tend to be resistant to change. Vested interests try to prevent it, and stability, predictability, and similar values argue in favor of leaving basic institutions alone. Whether a system such as that of the USSR can ultimately show itself sufficiently flexible to adjust to new needs remains to be seen. Meanwhile, its achievement should by no means be underestimated.

CHAPTER 8

Soviet Ideology: The Self-Image of the Soviet Union

The self-image of the Soviet state, which developed under Stalin and has, since then, undergone only minor modifications, is also to a large extent the official self-image of other communist societies, especially those of Eastern Europe. Hence it is to some extent the model on which the official ideology of most other communist states is based.

According to official Soviet rhetoric, the USSR no longer is a proletarian dictatorship but has turned into a socialist state of all those who work, or a state of all the people, in which exploitation and the class struggle have disappeared together with private property in the means of production. It is a state governed in accordance with a constitution that is more democratic than any other constitution past or present, because government is more truly representative of the people, and the rights of citizens are guaranteed more meaningfully than anywhere else.

After the completion of the Second Five-Year Plan, in the mid-thirties, the Soviet regime announced that the USSR had become a socialist society. It based this claim on the assertion that private enterprise had been eliminated completely with the abolition of the NEP and the collectivization of agriculture. Since production now proceeded according to a national plan presumably based on the needs of society rather than on the demands of the market—since, in other words, commodity production had been abolished—socialism was established by definition. This did not mean that the final goal of the communist movement had been reached. That final goal is communism, and party doctrine follows Lenin in making a careful distinction between socialism and communism. Communism is understood to incorporate the following features: an economy sufficiently productive to satisfy the material needs of all citizens and thus free them from material want; absolute equality of rewards, with the understanding that individuals will have different needs and different interests— equality of rewards then comes to mean the opportunity for every citizen freely to satisfy his or her own personal needs; universal rationality, or, as Soviet terminology expresses it, conscious- ness—a state in which all citizens have been raised to the level of consciousness hitherto attained only by the most advanced indi- viduals, the vanguard; a universal collective conscience which persuades every citizen to work freely and cheerfully, and without expectation of reward, for the collective good—under communism, Lenin said, unrewarded work for the community will have become a habit.

All these traits of communism imply that it is also without classes. All work will have become so mechanized that it will have turned into a routine everyone can perform. Or perhaps it will be so light a burden that people will be able to become skilled in many tasks. In any event, no longer will the division of labor divide people. In particular, all production will have become so mechanized or "automatized" that the differences between in- dustry and agriculture, between city and country, will have been wiped out. Finally, under communism, institutions of domina- tion will have become superfluous. Rule of some over others will have given way to the "administration of things" and to genuine collective self-government—the state will have withered away. In the late 1950s and early 1960s, when this question was discussed a great deal, the authorities were always careful to add that even then, however, the party would not wither away; presumably, the citizenry would still be divided into those of higher as against those of lower consciousness.

Of all the features attributed to final communism, voluntary work and equality of reward tend to be singled out, by Soviet doc- trine, as the principles ones, for communism is defined as a social order governed by the principle, "From each according to his ability; to each according to his need."

Socialism, in contrast, is the society that once the capitalists have been expropriated, sets out to reach that final goal, communism, by means of economic growth and the education of the people for communism. By definition, therefore, this is a society in which abundance is not yet produced. But if there are wants or needs that remain unfilled, there is no equality of unfulfillment or misery. Since voluntary work for the common good has not yet become the habit of every healthy organism, incentives are still required to make people work. Incentives, however, imply a system of managed inequality, the exact amount of the rewards (in material goods, status, power, or other values) to be determined by the individual's performance or his or her value to the community. And so socialism is defined as that system which is functioning according to the principle, "From each according to his ability; to each according to his work."

The need for incentives (and, as we shall see, sanctions) gives this socialism some similarity with capitalist and precapitalist societies. Under feudalism, the main incentive was the *knout*—whoever did not perform to the satisfaction of the lord was whipped. Under capitalism, the main incentive was hunger—whoever did not compete successfully in the labor market starved to death. The Soviet system also threatens its citizens with hunger if they do not pitch in; it has written this threat into its constitution, which contains the biblical words, "He who does not work, neither shall he eat," and makes them a guiding principle for Soviet society. At the same time, Soviet theory claims that the principal incentive under socialism is the expectation of greater reward, and, even more important, the desire for personal growth. Soviet citizens compete with each other not for the purpose of cutting each other's throats but in order to become more useful and more productive citizens. Soviet theory thus assumes a considerable amount of altruism, or perhaps more correctly, of enlightened self-interest, because the expectation of reward is supported by the conviction that labor for the collectivity is labor for one's self. Since private property in the means of production has yielded to public ownership, individuals working for the government or the society are in fact working for themselves, and the harder they work and the less reward they receive, the more quickly will they benefit from the general economic growth resulting from each individual citizen's labor and deprivation. Thus, while rewarding those who produce above the general norm or who have scarce skills, the Soviet government expects its citizens in general to postpone gratification of their material needs for the sake of raising the common level of production.

Until the early 1930s, the Soviet regime tended to be apologetic about the resulting differences in reward and regard them as a temporary emergency measure. As a matter of fact, in the first years after the revolution, it had tried to foster equality as much as possible and especially to prevent party members and government officials from profiting materially from their positions of authority. While these measures to level society down to an equality of misery were never entirely successful, they worked within limits, and the rhetoric of equality prevailed for about fifteen years. Since then, Soviet theory has taken a more positive attitude toward differences in material reward and has denounced "equality mongering" as a petit-bourgeois deviation from, and a betrayal of, socialist ideas—as something hostile to Soviet socialism. Indeed, a persuasive argument has been made to the effect that consumerism is now considered a virtue, that striving for comforts and material advancement is regarded as the proper aim of the self-respecting Soviet citizen.

A very similar change in doctrine must be noted in a closely related problem—the differentiation in authority possessed by the citizens. Lenin's statement that after the Revolution any female cook could take a turn at running the government was abandoned very quickly. But for a decade and a half after 1917 there was a cult of equality and a distrust of authority and rank, which may be explained in part by the fact that the individuals in positions of authority often were former tsarist officers or "bourgeois specialists" such as engineers and managers. To some extent, also, the cult of equality was a reaction against the age-old Russian tradition of rank consciousness, which had pervaded military and civilian life. One of the features of early Soviet administration, the custom of managing public agencies by committees, was clearly a result of this revulsion against authority as such. This egalitarianism, too, was now abandoned and denounced. It gave way to an authoritarian principle of individual leadership (*edinonachalie*), after Stalin announced that in Soviet society "cadres decide everything." The principle of hierarchy in command and authority was thus made part of the definition of socialism.* (I alluded to this reemergence of old Russian patterns of deference and rank-consciousness at the end of the preceding chapter.)

Did the claim that socialism had been achieved imply that Soviet Russia had become a classless society? By no means. Classlessness is attributed only to the final stage, communism. Then did this mean that a class struggle was still raging in the socialist society? Again the answer is no. To be sure, two different classes are acknowledged to exist, classes that have different interests and different relations to the means of production. One of these is the working class (no longer called proletariat, because a proletariat is defined as the class exploited by capitalism); the other one is the peasantry. Out of both classes, who are said to be held together by a firm and friendly alliance, rises an additional group, not a class, but only a stratum. This is the intelligentsia, which in Soviet terminology denotes all who are not workers or peasants. That means all white-collar and professional people, from clerks and typists to movie stars, generals, and cabinet ministers. The existence of these classes (plus one stratum) is thus acknowledged, and hence the existence of different class interests and class consciousness. But a conflict of classes is not admitted. Soviet theory asserts that the interests of these classes do not conflict, that class harmony and class collaboration characterize Soviet socialist society. For even though there are differences, these differences are not as deep as class differences in capitalism, because no class owns the means of production. No class exploits another class. There is no leisure class; all Soviet citizens—workers, peasants, and intelligentsia—are "toilers."

There is yet another distinction Soviet theory makes among its citizens. That is a distinction between the toilers on the one hand and the most advanced members of the working class, who make up the membership of the Communist party, on the other. The party is considered the most advanced organization of Soviet society because it knows the real interests of the workers, speaks

---

*"Cadres decide everything" was said by Stalin in May of 1935. See "Struktura otdela rukovodiashchikh partiinykh organov Ts. K. partii," *Partiinoe Stroitel'stvo*, No. 17 (1935), pp. 73–78.

for them, leads them, and represents them in word and in deed. The party is credited with outstanding accomplishments. It has led the Soviet people to emancipation from feudal and capitalist oppression, and it now provides guidance and supervision to Soviet citizens in all their endeavors. The membership of the party comprises the most conscious and advanced persons in every type of Soviet organization and in every walk of life. The party has always guided the Soviet people faultlessly, always accurately analyzing existing problems and situations, always correctly interpreting the interests of the people and finding the proper means toward the implementation of these interests. It has succeeded in this even though at times hostile elements have managed to worm themselves into the ranks of the party, even into very high places. Moreover, Marxism, which guides the party in its actions, is not easily mastered; while the party leadership has never wavered in the correct application of Marxist methods, even well-meaning members have at times deviated to the left or the right, succumbing either to the lure of antirevolutionary traitors or to the unproletarian influence of their own petit-bourgeois background. Whether or not such deviation is conscious, or willful, or based on evil intentions, objectively it makes the deviant member a counterrevolutionary. But the party has always saved its integrity by eliminating counterrevolutionaries. In recent years, it has been admitted further that in some matters even the party leadership went astray: Under Stalin, it fell victim to the "cult of personality" and allowed the General Secretary, now admitted to have been a criminal and a lunatic, to arrogate excessive power to himself, allegedly in violation of party principles. This led to grave and dangerous "mistakes," but wherever possible, these mistakes have been corrected; wiser because of the experience, the party will not fall into this error again. Soviet theory does not make it clear, however, what guarantees there are against the revival of the personality cult, nor has it made any attempt to find out how a man of Stalin's negative qualities could ever have acquired such supreme authority.

This, then, is the social structure of Soviet socialism, according to Soviet doctrine. It is a dynamic society, moving steadily toward all the transformations still required to bring about communism. The party expects to achieve this final goal within the foreseeable future. Several details of the process by which it expects to achieve it are worthy of our attention.

For one thing, Soviet doctrine asserts that the leap from socialism to communism will be made without a revolution. It will indeed be a leap, but it will be made as a result of gradual cumulative changes, and it will require neither the violent overthrow of an existing social order nor a system of domination. In Soviet socialist society, the superstructure does not lag behind the development of the forces of production, as it does in all other societies. It does not therefore get in the way of economic progress. On the contrary, it is a major agent of progress, and the last of the great Russian revolutions was the work of the Soviet government. This last revolution was the forcible elimination of *kulaks* and NEP people—the abolition of private enterprise—and it was a "revolution from above." Still, the Bolshevik revolution, according to Soviet theory, aligned the superstructure with the base, it still is a superstructure, and as we know, this must disappear under full-fledged communism. Left-wing critics of the Stalin regime in the early 1920s postulated a "third revolution" that would have to remove the superstructure. Soviet theory, however, seems to assume that the superstructure will simply wither away after it has done its job fully.

Marxism in its original form incorporated a theory of lag; the relations of production and the superstructure of traditions, mores, institutions, and ideologies growing out of these relations lagged behind the development of productive forces and became an obstacle to further progress. In Soviet doctrine, this relationship has been reversed. Soviet theory concedes that there is some lag; for instance, the continued maintenance of some private property in farming and of cooperative private enterprise in various crafts is regarded as a hangover from the capitalist past that sooner or later must be removed in order to align the relations of production with the productive forces. But, in the main, consciousness as well as social relations in Soviet socialism are regarded as being ahead of the development of the forces of production and as instruments to help build them up. The party's main tool in this is the *state*, which therefore acquires positive value as a force of progress. Formerly, the state was seen as a product of class struggle. Now there is no class struggle, according to Soviet theory, even though a conflict of interests is still acknowledged, such as the conflict between the individual's "immediate" and "real" interests. Some communists argued that therefore there was no justification for the state. But the party rejects this argument. We shall discuss the main grounds for this rejection below. Here we note only that the party justifies the state as an essential instrument for planning, organizing, and managing some of the transformations necessary to bring about the transition to communism, especially the growth of the forces of production. The state is the entrepreneur of socialism. By promoting production, it creates the preconditions for its own withering away. Soviet theory indignantly rejects the idea that the Soviet state might have become, or might in the future become, the instrument of rule for a privileged elite. Instead, it asserts (without being about to prove this except by tautological definitions) that the contradictions of Soviet society, including the clash between rich and poor, powerful and subordinate, will never entrench themselves and that the privileged elite express the common interest. While the capitalist state is the product of class antagonisms that it then helps to perpetuate, the Soviet state will resolve class antagonisms by increasing production.*

Additional agents of change and progress, according to Soviet doctrine, are *criticism and self-criticism*, as well as *socialist morality*—in short, the individual's intellectual awareness of his or her own shortcomings and those of fellow citizens, the free discussion of these failings in communal meetings and in media of mass communication, and the moral determination to overcome them and contribute to the best of one's ability, to be loyal and patriotic and confident of ultimate success. Failures in the Soviet system, poor performance of individuals or organizations, even criminality, neurosis, and insanity, according to Soviet theory, can usually be explained by the inadequate consciousness

*Against this, a growing number of analysts assert that Soviet society, like all modern industrial societies, is bound to develop into a stratified class society in which the industrial managers will sooner or later obtain control because they control the essential means of production. Developed as early as 1918 by the Polish socialist Waclaw Machajski, this theme was later picked up by James Burnham, *The Managerial Revolution* (New York, 1941), and repeated, with slight modifications, by Georg Achminov, *Die Macht in Hintergrund* (Ulm, 1950) and Milovan Djilas, *The New Class* (New York, 1957). The thesis is related to the pessimistic theories of both Roberto Michels and Leon Trotsky about inevitable bureaucratic perversions of socialism. Among contemporary Western Marxists this has by now become a widely accepted thesis.

or insufficient morality of some members of society. What else could be their cause, since the system itself is beyond criticism? Moreover, Soviet psychology assumes that all people are basically equal—not to believe this would be to succumb to myths about race and heredity. But if all human beings are equally endowed with intellectual and physical potentialities, differences in performance can be explained only by differences in will and application.

One of the cornerstones of Soviet doctrine was the concept of *socialism in a single country*. We remember that the Bolsheviks seized power in the firm expectation that the Russian Revolution would lead to proletarian revolutions in the entire civilized world. We have indicated why they expected this and why without world revolution their own success made little or no sense to them. In signing the Treaty of Brest-Litovsk, the Soviet regime chose coexistence with capitalism, but it did so only in the belief that the world revolution was still developing and needed only a chance to "catch its breath." After the abortive German revolutions of 1921 and 1923, it became clear to many Soviet leaders that the world revolution was going to take its time. The Communist International in its 1924 congress decided that world capitalism had entered a period of stabilization and that the world as a whole was in a transitional period between the Russian Revolution and the world revolution, a period during which the Soviet regime would have to coexist with the capitalist countries and find a *modus vivendi* with them.* Some members of the party pointed out that in this case the revolution would have been in vain, a senseless and costly adventure likely to discredit the Marxist movement as a whole. The Trotsky faction countered the doctrine of the stabilization of capitalism first by denying it and then by calling for vigorous revolutionary action on a global scale. They argued that the stabilization of capitalism was a passing phenomenon and that excessive attention paid to it amounted to opportunism and a betrayal of the revolution. Instead of adjusting to the ephemeral prosperity and stability of the capitalist world, the party should prepare for the new revolutionary upheavals that would inevitably accompany the equally in-

---

*Coexistence does not necessarily mean *peaceful* coexistence; Lenin's theories also contain the idea of an inevitable clash between the "camps" of capitalism and socialism, and he described the entire transition period between capitalism and socialism as an era of world wars and revolutions.

evitable end of stabilization. Not only that, the party ought to do its share to undermine capitalism and thus to promote and speed up the development of a new revolutionary situation. Here we have the global aspect of Trotsky's theory of "permanent revolution."

Against the arguments of the Trotsky faction the Stalin-Bukharin faction developed its theory of socialism in one country. They conceded that the revolution could never be completed, nor any of its achievements be safe, before the entire world (or a large portion of it) had become communist. But even though the achievements of the revolution would not be safe as long as they remained isolated in one country, this was no reason for despair. Even under such limiting conditions, socialism could be built in a single country, even a backward country like Russia. And to deny this possibility, they said, was defeatism and Menshevik pusillanimity. To be cowed by economic conditions or to emphasize the immaturity of any society for socialism, they argued, was shallow determinism. For a Bolshevik, social and economic conditions are not insurmountable obstacles but a spur to action. There is nothing that resolute action by the party cannot overcome.

With the victory of Stalin, the doctrine of socialism in a single country became party dogma, and with it the idea that a long transition period comes between the Russian Revolution and the completion of the world revolution. Two main implications were inherent in this: the recognition of *coexistence* as an inescapable necessity for the duration of the transition period, and the admission that socialism confined to one country (and a "backward" one at that) would look different from what the revolutionaries of 1917 had imagined and hoped it would look. These two implications were closely related to each other, the former being responsible for the latter. For it was a central point in Soviet theory to blame the exigencies of coexistence (termed "capitalist encirclement") for any disappointing features of Soviet socialism. In particular, capitalist encirclement was cited as the main reason why the state has not yet withered away, as a Marxist ought to have expected once he or she was told that exploitation and the class struggle had been abolished. Indeed, once the party had announced that socialism had been reached, party members seem to have queried whether the state could now be expected to wither away. In answering with a decided no, the party stressed capitalist encirclement but also alleged that coexistence had its domestic equivalents too, in that some elements of Soviet society were still susceptible to insidious capitalist influence from outside. A strong state, including a mighty army and a police force, was thus required to keep capitalism at bay, and the stronger it was made, the more quickly and surely would it wither away.* While Soviet theory thus made coexistence responsible for repressive features of Soviet society, Marxists who are antagonistic to the USSR have argued that the repressive nature of Soviet society is responsible for coexistence. The revolution occurred first in a country not mature for socialism. Whether this is to be blamed on Bolshevik adventurism or whether it was unavoidable is controversial. In any event, in a backward country only a sad caricature of socialism could be developed. This, it is argued, has so discredited revolutionary Marxism as a whole that it has perverted the normal course of history and enabled capitalism to entrench itself in the Western world, where true socialism might otherwise have been created after a proletarian revolution.

Soviet theory does not acknowledge the need to be apologetic about anything. True, the state has not yet withered away. But it is, after all, a most acceptable state, a constitutional democracy of a superior type, in which democracy is not just a phrase but a reality. Government by soviets, it is claimed, is the most ideal form of representative democracy because it gives the common people a better chance for direct control of, or participation in, the process of government than any other institution. Being a sensitive barometer of public opinion, Soviet government institutions allegedly do not require checks and balances or a division of powers. Soviet government is good government, and good government ought not to be curbed by such devices.

The Soviet constitution, it is claimed further, fulfills liberal ideals by being a federal constitution. The Union of Soviet Socialist Republics is a voluntary federation of free nations, each

---

*Herbert Marcuse in *Soviet Marxism* (New York, 1958), pp. 51–55, rightly points out that this is a theory of containment: According to Soviet theory, imperialism seeks to destroy the world revolution. He has shown that, despite modifications and reservations in their theory, the actual strategy of world communism has always presupposed that the revolution in the West had little chance, and that communist action should always be on the defensive.

one of which is at liberty to determine its own national destiny, even to the point of seceding from the USSR. That in fact this destiny consists in merging with the other nations making up the Soviet Union is taken for granted by Soviet theory, and anyone actually advocating secession from the Union would at once be recognized as an enemy of proletarian internationalism, and dealt with accordingly. The liberties granted by the most democratic of all constitutions are meaningful only as long as they are not abused by the class enemy.

In addition to providing self-determination for all nations of Soviet society, the constitution provides the individual citizens with basic rights. It grants not only the customary freedoms of speech, assembly, the press, and religious belief; it also outlaws discrimination based on sex, race, religion, or national origin. And, finally, it grants all citizens the right to employment, to an education, and to medical and other assistance in case of need. It thus complements political rights with social and economic rights.

Soviet theoreticians point out that, unlike all previous constitutions, the Soviet constitution also provides guarantees for these rights and thus makes them meaningful. What good is the capitalist freedom of the press to the workers who do not have the money to start a newspaper or run a television station? How valid is the freedom of assembly in societies where club houses or meeting halls are for hire or purchase only to those who are able to pay? In the USSR these and other rights and liberties are guaranteed by the fact that assembly halls and media of mass communication, as well as all the means of production, have been taken away from the capitalists and are now in the hands of the party and other organizations representing the will of the people, just as Soviet democracy is made truly representative by the fact that its informal processes, such as the nominations and selection of candidates for public office, are largely in the hands of the party, the trade unions, and other organizations expressing the interests of the toilers.

According to Soviet doctrine, the USSR is not only the most democratic state in the world, it is also the chief defender of democracy in international affairs. Lacking aggressive tendencies, the Soviet Union since its inception has consistently played a progressive role in world politics. Therefore, it is supported loyally not only by almost all its own citizens but also by all truly class-conscious workers in the world.

In the 1960s Soviet ideology for a while turned its attention to the problem of the transition from socialism to communism. We have noted that this was to take the form of a gradual, nonviolent transition. In his last essay, published shortly before the Nineteenth Congress of the party, Josef Stalin spelled out some of the preconditions for this transition. Communism would come within sight once the Soviet economy was able to raise real wages for the entire population to a specified level—and by extrapolating the rate of growth from records of Soviet productivity, economists could estimate that communism was still a few decades away. Further, Stalin postulated a major transformation of the collective farms before communism could be placed on the agenda, and a number of other conditions. On the basis of Stalin's calculations, the prospect of attaining communism in the near future receded. In retrospect, Stalin's conclusion can be interpreted as manifesting a conservative attitude. Stalin obviously meant to imply that any deviation from his own methods of government would be premature; the time was not yet ripe for any major changes. Some of his successors became more optimistic. Nikita Khrushchev announced several times that Soviet society was entering the stage of gradual transition from socialism to communism. In particular, he asserted that the state had already begun to wither away, and to support this assertion he referred to various measures taken by his regime to decentralize administration, place some functions of government in the hands of neighborhood groups and other grass-roots agencies, and curb the powers of the political police. Khrushchev's successors, in contrast, have seemed eager to play down the theme of the transition of communism.

Here and there, in passing, we have noted differences between the Soviet theory of state and the spirit of Marxist thought. We have even ventured to state that Soviet theory is in decided opposition to the humanist ethics and the radical criticism inherent in Marxism. Soviet theoreticians would not, of course, agree with this. They would assert that the history of the Russian Revolution, the development of Soviet society, and the doctrines of Soviet ideology are all in full correspondence with Marxist ideas. To make Marxism fit Soviet history and ideology, it has been transformed in the USSR into a dogmatic philosophy bearing some striking similarities both to Thomist philosophy and to the scientific clichés of the Victorian age. Its more abstract branch, corresponding to what Western philosophers would call ontology, epistemology, logic, and the philosophy of science or nature, is called "dialectical materialism." The parts dealing with anthropology and psychology, ethics, aesthetics, and the philosophy of history are called "historical materialism." In both branches, a catechism of philosophical laws has been abstracted from the writings of Marx, Engels, Lenin, and Stalin, laws that are said to describe the nature of all phenomena, social as well as nonsocial, in the universe. This philosophy affirms the objective reality of all phenomena and characterizes this reality as capable of being known by humans. It defines the substance of all reality as matter and ascribes to all material phenomena certain dynamic qualities, such a contradictoriness and motion, or change. Dialectical materialism further spells out the patterns of interrelationships between material phenomena, such as the multiple chain of causality relating all phenomena to each other, but especially the laws of motion of matter, or, as we might say, the morphology of change. As for historical materialism, it is a catechism of the most general assumptions and methods used by Marx, Engels, Lenin, and Stalin in describing and analyzing social phenomena.

Marx, and even more Engels, manifested positivistic tendencies amounting to a rejection of philosophy. Soviet philosophy opposes this positivistic attitude. It does not follow Engels in identifying philosophy with the method of natural and social science, nor restrict it to logic and the history of ideas. Instead, it recognizes philosophy as a branch of learning distinct from natural and social science, even though the boundaries between philosophy and science have never been satisfactorily defined. The result of this dualism is that scientific pursuits are, as it were, made subservient to, or brought into line with, philosophical dogma, in a fashion comparable to the manner in which the Church subordinates the rational pursuit of knowledge to the acceptance of revealed truth. In both cases scientific findings are recognized as valid only as long as they do not conflict with the established dogma. Also, in both cases it is taken for granted that the independent, rational search for scientific truth cannot possibly come into conflict with the dogma.

Soviet theory expresses this relationship in somewhat oblique fashion by asserting that all science is, and must be, partisan, or in line with the spirit of the party. This conformance to the party's policies and beliefs is called *partiinost'*. Its imposition on everyone engaged in intellectual pursuits is justified by the party in the following manner: All knowledge, they argue, is the reflection or expression of some class interest. In all fields of knowledge, therefore, there are feudal, bourgeois, petit-bourgeois, and proletarian schools. There cannot be any neutrality. Even those who believe they are neutral or who think that their fields of endeavor are far removed from politics will in fact ("objectively") reflect the point of view of one or another class. Now Marx has shown, according to Soviet arguments, that the class consciousness of the proletariat is true consciousness, whereas the consciousness of all other classes is false, ideological. Only in the consciousness of the proletariat does class interest lead to the emergence of truth unvarnished and undistorted. It follows from this that in every field of knowledge the search for truth will be successful only as long as the scholar wholeheartedly adopts the point of view of the working class. And since this point of view is expressed best by the Communist party, no scientific truth can stand that conflicts in any way with the party's views, the party line. Science, social as well as natural, including the purest research in physics, biology, or mathematics, must be pervaded with the spirit of *partiinost'*. In effect, this means that in any realm of knowledge where the party has expressed a definite opinion, it has been, until fairly recently, virtually impossible to engage in discussion with Soviet scholars because, imbued with *partiinost'*, they could not deviate from the accepted line or even the accepted terminology and were obliged to label any disagreement with their views or their vocabulary as the ideology of the class enemy. Thus scientific truth could not be pursued freely, and truths conflicting with the party line are declared falsehoods. As a result, more than one branch of Soviet science suffered lasting damage. But what we have said applies with particular force in the social sciences, where the party line was refined and defined with so much precision that it seemed to consist of inflexible magic formulas—a catechism or a litany that, according to Marcuse, did in fact function as magic, or to say the least, social science was used for the purposes of public relations, and the principles of advertising are in eternal conflict with the search for truth. Where the inflexible formulas developed in social science are changed ever so slightly, we must always suspect changes in party policy or party views.

Soviet ideology thus serves as an esoteric code of communications easily read by the initiated but decipherable also by the informed outsider.

The transformation of theory into catechism was not, however, restricted to the social sciences but applied also in the more "remote" areas of knowledge and ideology. The reason for this is simple. If we are right in asserting that Soviet social theory served mainly to obscure and veil the clash between the idea and the reality of socialism, if its dogmas were to pervert the ideals of liberty, equality, and fraternity by affirming that socialism had been attained, then the ideals thus perverted or betrayed would tend to retreat into the "inner emigration" of seemingly remote and neutral areas—art, philosophy, and science. But here too they are dangerous to the regime, and the party has tried very hard to ferret them out. There is therefore no safe place for an inner emigration in the Soviet Union, at least not in the intellectual realm.

Lest this picture be considered one-sided and overdrawn, we should, perhaps, add two qualifications. First, despite the tendencies just described, there have been some branches of social science in which respectable scholarly work has always been done. Even when speaking of the Stalin period, therefore, we should not underestimate the ability of Soviet social scientists to engage in significant research. But a second point that concerns the erosion of dogma, or at least of dogmatic rigidity, in Soviet intellectual life is more important. We have already mentioned this loosening up, but we should add now that in recent years the pace of this process seems to have speeded up considerably. If some years ago we could say that the higher ranks of the party were allowed freedom of discussion (though not yet freedom of speech), it now appears that it is practiced far more widely and far more openly than Western scholars would have believed possible twenty years ago. An ever widening range of problem areas in the administration of the country are openly, publicly discussed, if not in daily newspapers and in other media of mass communication, then at least in professional journals. The tone in which problems are analyzed often is free from ideological jargon. Both in method and in vocabulary Soviet administration and Soviet social science have obviously come under the influence of corresponding scholarship in the West; the writings of Soviet specialists in a host of fields often is indistinguishable from analogous

European or American works. In addition, the portrayal of Soviet life and its problems in fiction, in film, and on the stage has become more open, if only by increments.

Precisely what these trends indicate is difficult to say. Are the reins of thought control loosened because the leadership itself is becoming more sophisticated and less strongly committed to the doctrines of Marxism-Leninism? Are they slackening their ideological controls because they have convinced themselves that, by and large, the Soviet population, especially in the younger generations, takes the system and its aims so much for granted that a somewhat freer discussion of problem areas no longer represents a threat? Of course, indoctrination goes on. As in every political system, the Soviet regime carefully socializes its citizens into adherents, and this socialization process everywhere starts in the cradle, continues through childhood into adulthood, and never stops. Every public event, every national holiday, every election is an occasion for displaying the visible symbols and mouthing the sacred truths of the reigning doctrine. But how much of this is routine, analogous to Fouth-of-July oratory, and of little more significance for daily life? And if indeed indoctrination has turned into empty sermonizing, is this an indication that the ideology now is firmly rooted in the minds of the people, or is it a sign that the roots are weakening? Only the future will give an answer.

CHAPTER 9

The Communist International, 1919–1943

When the Russian Bolsheviks seized power in 1917, they firmly expected that their deed would spark proletarian revolutions in the advanced countries of Western Europe. Most of them thought that without world-wide revolution the establishment of a communist regime in a country such as Russia made no sense whatever. Socialism, in their minds, presupposed a high stage of industrial development and a numerous, politically mature working class that could use this industrial establishment in rational fashion so as to ensure material plenty for all. In any society not providing these conditions, the erection of a socialist government was thought to be a premature and dangerous adventure. Either the socialist party would be overthrown very quickly, running the risk of total annihilation by the victorious counterrevolution, or if against all odds it maintained itself in power, it could do so only by catering to the interests of a population not yet receptive to a Marxist program. The proletarian regime would turn into a sad caricature of itself and greatly discredit the whole Marxist movement.

And yet the Bolsheviks seized power. Compelled by the traditions of their own movement to do nothing that did not correspond to Marxist prognoses or could not be fitted into Marxist programs of action, their leaders had to assume that the world revolution was around the corner and that the productive potential of a socialist Europe would secure the gains made by the revolution in Russia. Not all Bolshevik leaders shared this confidence—those who did not hotly argued against seizing power—but those who did must not be regarded necessarily as utopian dreamers or reckless adventurers. On the contrary, there were many indications in 1917 that Europe was on the brink of revolution. A disastrous war had ruined its economies and shaken its regimes. Troops in France, Italy, and Germany had mutinied. Grave political unrest had made itself felt despite wartime censorship and emergency military rule. Where such indications were absent, their own theory told those around Lenin that a revolution *had* to be in the making as a result of the war. They all took for granted that this would be a proletarian revolution ushering in socialism, just as Marx and Engels on the eve of 1848 had taken for granted that the coming revolution would inevitably be transformed into a proletarian one.

The Bolshevik hopes were disappointed. The Russian Revolution remained isolated and, only a few months after the October uprising, had to adjust to the disappointing need for coexistence with capitalism by signing a peace treaty with Imperial Germany. To be sure, in signing this document, Lenin and his associates thought that they were only buying time sufficient for the world revolution to catch its breath. But the short breather extended to decades, and the very same arguments that had rationalized coexistence for but a little while came to sanction it for a long period. Rationalizing coexistence, however, meant rationalizing the pursuit of a policy devised to secure the survival of the Soviet state. Coexistence therefore meant the emergence of a Soviet national interest or *raison d'état*, the pursuit of which was said to coincide with the interests of the proletarian world revolution.

Still, by opting for coexistence, the Russian communists had not meant to abandon the cause of the world revolution. On the contrary, they signed their peace treaty with a capitalist power only so that the revolution might be given a chance to get under way. The war was still going on, after all, and in their eyes the world was still on the very brink of proletarian revolution. And indeed, even when the military conflict ended in November of 1918, the vehement economic, social, and political disturbances ensuing in the wake of the war lasted for another five years, keeping alive the most ambitious communist hopes.

During the war, Lenin had demanded that a new International be formed to replace the Second International, that world-wide federation of socialist parties which the war had destroyed. He had been exasperated by the leaders of these parties when with little hesitation they decided to support the war effort of their governments and thereby showed that national loyalty was stronger than their feeling of solidarity with the proletarians of all countries. In Lenin's eyes they were traitors to the cause of the proletarian revolution, and he was determined not to be associated with them any longer. A revival of an international organization of working-class parties there must be, but definitely without any of the leaders who in his opinion had no place in, and could not contribute anything to, the party of the international proletariat. There were many socialists leaders who, like Lenin, regretted the collapse of international working-class solidarity and who joined him in criticizing the leaders of the European socialist parties, yet many of them were hesitant to perpetuate the gulf that had opened between revolutionaries and moderates. Instead, they were eager to repair solidarity by trying to resurrect the international organization that had crumbled in 1914. Lenin's scorn of these people was as vehement as his hatred of the moderates.

Early in 1919 a congress of radical socialists assembled in Moscow to create the new International Lenin had demanded. The time seemed propitious. True, the Spartacus uprising in Germany had just been drowned in blood. But Hungary and Bavaria were in the hands of communist governments. Revolts against Western rule seemed to be brewing in the Near and Far East. All of Europe was in the throes of a violent postwar crisis. Still, the parties or factions represented, or purporting to be represented, at the founding congress were as yet without substantial following or even organization. Some delegates were extremely hesitant to help create an international socialist organization designed for the express purpose of keeping out the majority of socialist leaders and organizations. They would have preferred a renewal of the old International. But Lenin was eager to go ahead precisely because he wanted to anticipate and forestall the revival of the Second International. He wanted to face international socialism with a *fait accompli* and thus force all socialists to take sides, either with the new international or against it. The statutes of the new organization, adopted by the Second Congress, in 1920, were designed to enforce this compulsion to choose by imposing conditions on every would-be member party designed to antagonize and eliminate all those desiring a compromise—the famous twenty-one conditions. In addition, these statutes had the effect of imposing Lenin's principles of organization on every member party and on the Third International as a whole. Moreover, since that organization was designed to facilitate the exercise of leadership or command over a disciplined political machine, the imposition of Leninist organization also spelled the imposition of Leninist (or Russian) policies on the Third International, since quite naturally the Russian communists, with their prestige as successful revolutionaries, dominated the top command of the International from the very beginning. The many communist parties that came into life after the creation of the International, and also the even more numerous auxiliary organizations in all the world, in this fashion became appendages of the Russian *apparat*, in organization as well as in policy.

From its very beginning up to its dissolution, the policies of the Communist International were confused by the ambiguity of its main aims. Ostensibly, its objective was to promote proletarian revolution everywhere and, as an auxiliary move, to promote colonial revolutions in areas dominated by Western powers. But the pursuit of this goal was complicated by the fact that all communist parties were also expected to support the national interests of the USSR, and these interests were not always easy to reconcile with the presumed interests of revolution making. In fact, the evidence strongly suggests that, at least in Europe, where the USSR tried very hard to coexist with the leading capitalist nations, the efforts of the Communist International and those of the Soviet Commissariat for Foreign Affairs constantly embarrassed and frustrated and negated each other. Western communists could not but be aware of the baneful influence of Soviet national interests over the policies of their parties. Nor were they entirely happy that Russia was the country that became the pathbreaker and model for the development of a proletarian revolution. This raw and uncouth land of illiterate peasants, governed with a mixture of inefficiency and oriental ruthlessness that repelled many visitors, was not really a very suitable advertising sign for Marxist communism—certainly not in the first two or three decades of its existence. On the contrary, it was in many ways a source of embarrassment for Western communists. Meanwhile, Western diplomats and bourgeois politicians, compelled by various reasons to seek friendly relations with the Soviet Union, could not, in their turn, help being aware (even if they had not been reminded constantly by their constituents) that Moscow was not only the capital of a state with which it was necessary to coexist but also the headquarters and planning center of an international revolutionary movement aiming at the overthrow of all bourgeois governments.

In Asia the incompatibility between Soviet foreign policy and the activities of the Communist International was not nearly so pronounced. In China, Afghanistan, Persia, and Turkey, Moscow was dealing with revolutionary regimes seeking to emancipate their countries from Western domination. Colonial revolution could be fitted into the policies of Soviet foreign relations as well as into the policies of world communism. And yet, on closer examination, difficulties abounded in this area of the world too. While communist theory sought to convert the colonial revolution into an ally and an auxiliary force of the Western proletarian revolution, strategies to promote this end had not been elaborated and were a matter of keen controversy. Questions concerning the aims that ought to be promoted in colonial revolutions and the objectives that ought to be set, the forces with which communist parties ought to, or might, ally themselves, the nature of such alliances and the very meaningfulness of communist parties in countries where no industrial proletariat existed—these and many similar problems faced the strategists of the Communist International. Many different methods were tried: occasional attempts to spread communism by force of arms; the founding of communist parties, which then sought a mass basis among the urban workers, the peasants, or even national and religious minorities and which were ever prone to be dismayed by Moscow's orders to ally themselves with other revolutionary parties. Furthermore, in order to aid the colonial revolution, Moscow (and it is not always clear whether Asian policy emanated from the International or from the Soviet Foreign Office) at times supported popular revolutionary parties or leaders, such as the Guomindang or Kemal, anti-Western princes such as Reza Pahlevi in Iran and Amanullah Khan in Afghanistan, or even feudal lords like Ibn Saud, as long as they were actively opposing the West (meaning especially Britain). Here too, therefore, considerations of foreign policy and revolution making came into conflict with each other, to the eventual detriment of both.

A further difficulty besetting the policies of the Comintern was the result of overcentralization. The International had been organized in the image of the Russian Communist party not only because its kind of organization made it into a centralized, disciplined striking organization. That pattern of organization was further rationalized by the assumption that the working classes everywhere are basically alike. When Marx and Engels in the *Communist Manifesto* said that the proletarians have no fatherland, they presupposed an international solidarity of workers who in their living conditions and problems, their thinking and their political goals, were more like each other than like the capitalists in their own countries. In short, Marx and Engels assumed that capitalism, fundamentally, was the same everywhere. Hence the possibility of an international, united proletarian movement. Lenin and his comrades subscribed to these views, and the Third International was organized so as to serve as the united, centralized Communist party of all proletarians everywhere.

On a very high level of abstraction, the view of the workers of the world as having certain problems and interests in common may have been defensible. But concretely (and that means also politically), it was a mistake. The working class of each country could, rather, be expected to have problems of its own and to fight its own capitalists with weapons and strategies attuned to its own special conditions. Moreover, while party ideologists viewing politics from the grandstand of long-range historical generalizations may convince themselves that workers in all countries have more in common with their fellow proletarians across the borders than with "their own" capitalists, workers in real life tend to be just as patriotic as other citizens; nationalism, perhaps the strongest force in the political life of the twentieth century, does not know class boundaries. If this is accepted, it will be clear that overcentralization and its corollary, the imposition of a unified policy line on the International, were a serious blunder that must have wrecked the chances of many a revolution.

Yet the programs and strategies of the various member parties were fitted to the Procrustean bed of the Comintern's world-wide party line. Resistance to any of the more disastrous decisions which this procedure imposed on the various parties was stifled and punished as a serious breach of discipline. Communist parties were ill equipped, therefore, to accommodate leaders who thought for themselves or who thought that conditions in their own countries demanded a special course of action. The rapid turnover of leaders in the Bolshevik party from its very beginnings therefore came to be a characteristic feature of the Communist International as well. The situation was not at all improved by the fact that disputes over policy were often intertwined with, or affected by, the struggle for power raging among the leaders. More specifically, conflicts within the Third International were closely tied to the bitter fights within the Russian party and were decided by the outcome of these fights, so that personnel turnover within the various member parties faithfully mirrored the personnel changes in the Russian party. Finally, for reasons discussed above, the various communist parties were unable to respond to the nationalist or patriotic sentiments of the workers they sought to attract. In many ways, the cards were stacked against the Comintern's becoming an effective promoter of any rational policy.

After all I have said, it should not astonish anyone that the Third International was one gigantic failure. It did not succeed in creating a single proletarian dictatorship or communist regime. Nor did it manage to preserve and strengthen many of the strong communist parties that had been created in the years after World War I, although some of these parties survived World War II or even emerged from it more numerous and influential than ever before. Finally, the Comintern must be considered a dismal failure in its efforts to shield the Soviet Union and promote its national interests. I shall try to support these generalizations by a brief survey of the history of the International.

In the first years after World War I, valuable time was lost in gathering experience and organizing. The creation of the Comintern required vigorous efforts to persuade all like-minded socialist leaders to split off from the more moderate parties to which they had belonged and to found communist parties conforming in organization and policy to the Russian model. Some of the member parties started out as small, insignificant sects. Others acquired a mass following fairly quickly, especially the Communist party of Germany (KPD), which soon became and for some years remained the center of the International's hopes. The new parties were as yet unsure of their goals and methods. In their sporadic attempts at promoting proletarian revolutions and seizing power they placed great reliance on organizers and leaders sent by Moscow, usually Russian or Hungarian comrades whose experience in real revolutions gave them tremendous prestige. Nonetheless, the first attempts at revolution were handled in amateurish fashion and ended in failure, as did the desperate attempt, made in 1920, at exporting revolution at bayonet point by conquering Poland. In the wake of these failures came not only the first purge of disobedient leaders but also the first major switch in the policy line of the Communist International: After the abortive communist revolution in Germany in 1921, the International abandoned such reckless adventures, decided that the major danger to the working-class movement lay in right-wing authoritarianism, and consequently adopted the policy of the "United Front" with the moderate socialists. In line with this policy, communist parties were enjoined to offer collaboration to moderate socialists, ostensibly for the purpose of safeguarding democratic institutions and workers' rights, but in reality with the aim of infiltrating socialist parties and more particularly trade unions. In China, which together with Germany was the main focus of Comintern hopes in these years, the new policy led to the alliance and actual merger of the Chinese Communist party with the Guomindang—a step which at the time was hailed with enthusiasm, though in the end it brought only disaster to the Chinese communists.

In Europe the policy of the United Front came to naught for several reasons. For one, the moderate socialists were generally in no mood to ally themselves with communist parties, especially since the communists themselves were frank enough to admit their desire to destroy or swallow up the moderates. Secondly, as the aftermath of World War I came to a dramatic climax, it seems that the rank-and-file membership of the communist parties became impatient with the moderate and cautious defensive policy that the United Front implied. While political and economic chaos engulfed Europe, the high command of the International and the leaders of the European parties were divided, and the top decision makers hesitated. In the end, an attempt to unleash revolution in Germany, which was finally made in October of 1923, was bungled and ended in disaster. Changes of personnel and policy followed as a matter of course.

Following the debacle of the "German October" in 1923, the Communist International settled down to the serious work of consolidating its substantial gains in Western and Central Europe. It found it possible to elaborate greatly its network of auxiliary organizations set up to organize and educate different groups in the population of the capitalist countries. A great deal of energy was also spent in the recurrent fights against opposing factions and, once the major oppositions had been eliminated, in making personnel changes that brought to the top disciplinarians and obedient spokesmen of the Kremlin, organization men who could not be expected to make any trouble. This change of personnel was called the "bolshevization" of the Comintern.

For serious revolution making, the time did not seem propitious. In Europe and in the New World, this was a period of "normalcy" and prosperity, which brought with it a flowering of constitutional democracy and middle-class culture. Sporadic outbursts of labor trouble, as for instance the British General Strike of 1926, did not yield any benefits to the communist parties. In Asia, national revolutions continued to break out. But in India, China, the Dutch East Indies, and elsewhere the communist parties did not succeed in playing major roles in these revolutions. To be sure, the Indian Congress Party contained a left wing headed by Jawaharlal Nehru, which found a good deal of inspiration in communist ideas, and similar intellectual currents were alive in other colonial countries. But they did not yield benefit to the communist parties. In China, the happy merger of the party with the revolutionary Guomindang was forcibly dissolved in 1926. "Comrade" Jiang Kaishek, officially still affiliated with the Comintern, decimated the ranks of the Chinese Communist party by a bloody purge and destroyed communist hopes for years to come. The years of prosperity ended with the Communist International better organized than ever—strong parties and a widely ramified network of auxiliary organizations, all of them in the hands of "safe" leaders. Although the period had not brought any more tangible political success, the leaders of international communism were confident that new trouble was brewing for the capitalist world and that the years of prosperity were coming to an end. From the coming depression, which they predicted accurately, the communist world expected the development of a new revolutionary situation that would take global proportions.

The Great Depression predicted by the Comintern came in 1929. It hit the capitalist world cruelly, ruined its economy, created mass unemployment and misery. It brought with it a general turn toward political radicalism, which in Eastern Europe, Germany, and France destroyed democratic constitutionalism. In the capitalist countries it was a time of profound crisis from which the Communist International might have benefited but did not. The general shortcomings of the Third International go far in explaining this. But some additional reasons must be mentioned. First of all, the Great Depression coincided with the first and second five-years plans in the Soviet Union, a time when Russia was busy with its own problems and its leaders were unwilling to trouble themselves with international complications. Revolution making was as far as it could be from the minds of the leaders in Moscow, who had plenty on their hands in trying to industrialize their country and control their population. The International in this period made a good deal of radical noise, but this was primarily to hide its actual policy of isolationism.

The radical rhetoric was a function of the new policy line adopted by the International at this time, a policy of uncompromising leftism. It should by now have become clear that one of the major problems of communist policy making has always been to define the attitude of the party to other socialist parties. Just as the communists are ambivalent in their appraisal of the working class itself, at times being confident that the proletariat has become "conscious," at times despairing over its lack of consciousness, so their judgment changes about parties that, like their own, purport to speak for the workers. To be sure, the Comintern was founded with the specific purpose of making the gulf between communists and social democrats unbridgeable. Lenin's own loathing of moderate socialism and its representatives was shared by his followers. And even when the International expressed the desire for an alliance between the two parties, the understanding was that the communists sought to support the socialists "as the noose supports the man who is being hanged." And yet, the actual policies of the Third International toward the moderate socialists were subject to considerable modifications. Whenever the Comintern was convinced that its very existence (or that of the USSR) was threatened by conservative or reactionary forces, it formed a defensive alliance with left-of-center liberals or moderate socialists, an alliance formed ostensibly to preserve constitutional democracy and the liberties associated with it. But its basic hostility toward the social democrats would break through in full force, particularly in periods when a revolutionary situation was believed to be developing. At such times, a communist had to be on guard against the socialists, because in the opinion of any communist they were, after all, only the left wing of the bourgeoisie, and they could be expected to betray the revolution. When the time for great decisions draws near, it is always the unreliable ally who becomes the most dangerous enemy and must be unmasked and opposed.

An so, when the Western world was staggering under the blows of the economic crisis, when constitutional democracy was eroded by radicalism of the right and the left, the communist parties concentrated their fire on the socialist parties. As a result, the Comintern achieved partial success: "Bourgeois democracy" in much of the Continental Europe was destroyed. But the communist parties did not manage to take the second step they had hoped and expected to take—to grab the power from the tottering capitalists. Instead, right-wing authoritarian regimes took over wherever constitutional democracy could not manage to maintain itself. These regimes came to power partly in the name of militant anticommunism, and once they were in power they usually proceeded to stamp out communism, together with the remnants of socialism and democratic liberalism. As a result, the most important communist parties outside the Soviet Union, together with some lesser ones, were destroyed almost completely. The vast political machinery of the Third International, built up with blood and tears and tremendous resources, was destroyed in one terrible blow.

Nor was the movement any more successful in the colonies and underdeveloped areas. In China, Comintern agents or Chinese leaders obedient to the commands of Moscow made futile attempts to stir up the urban masses. They were defeated by the lethargy of the workers, by the Guomindang, and by the Japanese invasion of Manchuria. Meanwhile, a little-known communist warlord, Mao Zedong, while paying lip service to Comintern instructions, silently began to build up the strength of the party on the basis of an overwhelmingly rural following—a pro-

letarian party without a proletariat. In the northwestern part of
China and also behind the lines of the Japanese (after they had occupied portions of China proper), substantial rural areas came
under the authority of this Communist party, so that, gradually
and without attracting much notice in Comintern circles, the nu-
cleus of a veritable communist republic developed.

A major reversal in policy was undertaken in 1935, not only as
a result of the defeats we have just discussed, but more directly
because of new international developments. By this time it had
become apparent that the Great Depression and the ensuing political crises would not lead to proletarian revolutions. Instead,
they had produced fascist and authoritarian regimes that were
not only militantly anticommunist but also militantly aggressive
in international relations. The Soviet Union felt itself threatened
by the clear and present danger of German and Japanese attacks.
More than ever its leaders were concentrating their attention on
the problems of economic and military growth and on instilling
unquestioning loyalty and discipline into its population. But they
also tried to secure themselves through action in the international
arena.

From the beginning, the foreign policy of the USSR relied primarily, though not exclusively, on the device frequently used by
powers that are weak and feel themselves threatened. This device is to seek allies among other weak, threatened, or dissatisfied
powers, so as to confront the major powers with a protective alliance of the underdogs. The underdogs, or have-not powers, with
whom Soviet Russia cultivated mutually fruitful relations on this
basis included Germany, Italy, Japan, China, Iran, and Turkey. It
should be noted that this policy was altogether unrelated to the
real pursuits of the Communist International. If anything, these
pursuits were in conflict with Soviet attempts to cement its alliances with the underdogs of the capitalist world of nations.

Now, in 1935, for the first time the policies of the International
were geared immediately to the Soviet's policy of alliances. Alarmed
by the military threat of German and Japanese power, Moscow's
satellite parties adopted the policy of the Popular Front. Communist parties everywhere sought to ally themselves with, or even
give unrewarded support to, any political group or government
ready to resist fascism, national socialism, or other forms of
government regarded as direct threats to the Soviet Union.

To be sure, attempts were made to use Popular Front arrangements or alliances to wean the masses away from moderate programs, to build up communist strength by taking command over
socialist or liberal groups of one sort or another and thus to prepare for proletarian revolution. As a consequence, a good deal of
ill feeling and distrust arose between the communist parties and
the groups they sought to use or abuse. But, in general, the International and its affiliated parties tended to tone down their specifically communist aims and programs. The communist parties
at least ostensibly transformed themselves into the left wing of
liberal and moderate socialist parties. They came out as defenders
of due process and constitutional government and, in international affairs, of collective security. The USSR entered the League
of Nations, which for years it had denounced as the victors' club
of the big imperialist states, and the Soviet spokesman, Maxim
Litvinov, acquired the reputation of being the staunchest defender of global democracy. The Soviet government and its satellite parties went to great pains to persuade the world that the
USSR itself was a thoroughly democratic country governed on
the basis of a liberal constitution. In his interview with Roy
Howard, in 1936, Stalin rejected the allegation that he or his government was interested in promoting world communism, a statement that, given his political career, was obviously ridiculous.
Yet Stalin at that moment may have meant what he said. At the
same time, the attempt to mobilize the forces of democracy
against fascism and similar movements was made by Moscow, at
least to some extent with the expectation that it would fail (and
would thereby reveal the hypocrisy of liberal democracy). Doubtless many communists preached liberal ideals only in order to
show that under capitalism these ideals cannot be fulfilled. Perhaps Litvinov's disarmament proposals and communist attempts
to safeguard civil liberties and constitutional democracy were
similarly motivated. But the first impetus for these attempts undoubtedly came from the threats of aggression facing the USSR.

In pursuit of the Popular Front policy, communist programs
were not only toned down, but in some cases deliberate steps
were actually taken to prevent or sabotage revolutions. In China,
for instance, the Popular Front policy compelled the communists
to ally themselves with their archenemy, Jiang Kaishek, against
Japan and even to save his life and liberty after he had fallen into

their hands through the kidnapping at Xi'an (Sian) in 1936. The Chinese communists did so only with the greatest reluctance, many of them doubtless feeling that Moscow was betraying them. In Spain, the party faced a dilemma—either to support and promote the working-class revolution that had begun and thereby endanger the war effort, or to deliberately postpone and stamp out the revolution for the purpose of winning the civil war. Without hesitation the party chose the latter course and lost both the war and the revolution. In the United States, the Popular Front policy caused the party to support the New Deal, even though they had at first denounced it as a semifascist attempt to save capitalism from certain collapse.

It should also be remembered that the years of the Popular Front coincided with the Great Purge in the Soviet Union. The Western world was being challenged to defend constitutional democracy just at the time when police terror was celebrating bloody orgies in the USSR. It was, moreover, a period of national frenzy and intense xenophobia in Russia, and whether by accident or design, foreign nationals were hit with especial ferocity by the purges. The Soviet Union, by this time, was the refuge of great numbers of foreign communists who had fled from political persecution in their own countries. These colonies of foreign communist leaders were decimated by the Great Purge, which virtually wiped out several communist parties. The work left unfinished by the Gestapo or similar institutions in Poland, Hungary, and other states was thus completed by the NKVD, the Soviet Political Police. Meanwhile, the entire purge orgy, with its open and secret trials, its fantastic confessions, had a chilling effect on many people in Western countries in sympathy with communism and so jeopardized the success of the Popular Front policy.

In the end, the Popular Front policy turned out to be as much of a failure as all previous Comintern policies. The communist parties did not succeed in making lasting alliances with any socialist parties, although numerous left-wing groups and associations in the Western democracies came under the influence of their new communist members (who had joined in obedience to Popular Front policy directives) and often voiced the party line. That line consisted of warnings against fascism, praises for liberal democracy, and assertions that the USSR in its domestic and foreign policies was the only country which consistently followed and promoted the ideals and precepts of liberal democracy, while in the Western democracies these ideals were being betrayed or in danger of being betrayed. Although some of these notions attained considerable popularity among intellectuals in England, France, the United States, and a few other countries between 1935 and 1938, the Communist International was unable to make these ideas pay off: The Western democracies did not yield to the prodding given them by Moscow and by their own left-of-center circles to resist German, Italian, or Japanese aggression. Instead, they followed the paths of "nonintervention" and "appéasement," which in the end led to the Munich pact of 1938. This pact marked the complete and utter failure of the Popular Front. Once again the Third International had miscalculated disastrously.

From this point on, it was a moribund organization. In response to Munich, the USSR signed a treaty of friendship with the Third Reich in August of 1939, dismaying and rebuffing sympathizers and fellow travelers in the West and also many party members, who had supported the USSR and the party as the staunchest bastions against fascist aggression. As England and France prepared to fight at last against Nazi Germany, the Communist International advised its followers that the new war was an imperialist war—a family quarrel between imperialist nations and of no concern to the party of the proletariat. Instead, the workers were urged to sabotage the war effort, to resist emergency controls and the imposition of wartime hardships, and to desert from the armed forces. The small number of people who heeded this call attested to the lack of influence any of the communist parties had among the masses.

The final reversal of Comintern policies was a natural consequence of Hitler's attack on the USSR in June of 1941. The Communist International automatically resumed the slogans of the Popular Front, this time with renewed vigor and with changes in emphasis. No longer was it necessary to goad the Western democracies into resistance to national socialism. Their will to resist was now assured, and if it needed to be revived occasionally, this was accomplished far more advantageously by the Soviet government, now allied with the democracies, than by the communist parties. These parties had only one more function left—to persuade their followers that the only task for faithful communists now was to support the allied war effort. Workers in the West were to forget their grievances against capitalists. They were to do their best and make no demands. Racial, religious, or national minorities feeling the sting of discrimination were to shelve their complaints for the duration of the war and forget about their aims to gain equality. Rebellious nationalists in the colonies were to forget or postpone their demands for freedom and self-government and give their full support to the governments they had always been told to regard as their oppressors. Communist resistance groups in countries occupied by the enemy were urged to merge with, and even subject themselves to, noncommunist resistance forces, to give up their identity and goals so as not to jeopardize the war effort or embarrass the Soviet Union.

It is obvious that instructions of this nature had not the slightest similarity to communist programs. Moreover, the USSR apparently regarded the very existence of the International as an embarrassment and a hindrance. In its efforts to cement the wartime alliance with the Western democracies, which Moscow considered essential for the successful defense of the Soviet Union, the Kremlin did not wish to remind its allies that it had once been the headquarters of the world revolution. That world revolution was not, for the time being, on the agenda. Consequently, without ceremony or fanfare, without even the pretense of going through elaborate formal procedures, the little side show or, as Stalin is reputed to have called the Communist International contemptuously, the "little shop" quietly closed its books and folded its tents. The year was 1943. It is ironic and perhaps significant that the international organization of communist parties was dissolved precisely at the time when for the first time since 1917 the international communist movement was about to achieve important gains. The battle of Stalingrad was the turning point of the war and of the history of the world in our century. The Soviet Union began to emerge as a major world power.

Equally important was the fact that a number of communist parties, working with greater independence from Moscow (because the war prevented communications and control), managed, *because* of this absence of control, to make important gains in size and influence. As a result of World War II and because of the demise of the Comintern, communism for the first time became an important world force.

It might be argued that some credit for this new success should be given to the Comintern and its Russian leadership, including Stalin. After all, it was this leadership which first built a world-wide communist movement, and it was its emissaries and agents who provided foreign communists with knowledge of revolutionary techniques. Against this, I submit that communist parties would have been created in many parts of the world in any event, and more spontaneously, even without the help of the Comintern. Indeed, they would most probably have been more closely attuned to their own political systems and would therefore have been more successful. Moreover, inventiveness in revolutionary techniques is no Russian monopoly, and we can safely assume that revolutionary leaders throughout the world would have acquired the necessary know-how without instructors from Moscow. The fact remains that wherever the Comintern remained in control, communist revolutions inevitably failed. The gains communism made after World War II were achieved despite the weight of Comintern history, and despite Stalin's leadership.

CHAPTER 10

Third World Communism

Until the end of World War II, the Soviet Union was the only country in the world governed by a party affiliated with the Communist International. But only a few years after the war, communists were in power in Eastern Europe, China, North Korea, North Vietnam, and Cuba; in subsequent years other Third World countries were to be added to this group.

Developments in Eastern Europe will be discussed in Chapter 11. Here let me make some observations about the development of communism in countries far less developed economically than even the poorest states of Eastern Europe.

We live in a profoundly revolutionary age, and perhaps the most spectacular element in the revolution of our time is the rise of the underdeveloped nations. When we study social sciences, we usually study the history, politics, and economics of Western Europe and North America. Our view of the world for centuries has been highly ethnocentric—for the nations of Asia, Africa, and Latin America did not seem to count. However populous, they were negligible because of their political, economic, and military weakness. They were objects of exploitation or domination, either as colonies or as dependencies or satellites. Whites ruled these countries through arrogant and arbitrary colonial administrators, military or civilian. Neither these officials nor the builders and traders and overseers who represented Western business were always the highest representatives of European civilization; on the contrary, service in the underdeveloped dependencies was often sought by highly unattractive personalities, people who, as Hannah Arendt has put it, had become superfluous in their own societies.

The West, however, brought not only domination by tactless, stupid, or ruthless colonial officials, not only new forms of economic exploitation for native labor; it also brought blessings: material wealth through the implantation of Western industrial enterprises, valuable technical and administrative skills for a small elite of cooperative natives. For those blessings, the people of Asia, Africa, and Latin America are not, as a rule, grateful to the West. On the contrary, one legacy of colonialism and dependency is an unbounded hatred of whites, who are remembered as the arrogant intruders, the tyrants, the barbarians who disrupted and destroyed the traditional way of life and even claimed gratitude for it.

Whatever these people's attitude toward the West, there is one other thing that white rule has brought to their countries, and that is revolution. Wherever they appeared, Western administration and Western commerce and industry disrupted old-established cultures, uprooting entire social classes. Christian missionaries meanwhile acquainted the native people with the idea of brotherly love, while Western educators sought to propagate democracy, free enterprise, nationalism, and socialism. With this education, the people of underdeveloped and dependent countries were given various directions for solving the problems the encroachment of the West had created for them. The lesson was that the colonial nations might improve their lot by applying Western ideas and ideals to their own societies.

The need for drastic action, for revolutionary transformation, which is felt by political leaders in underdeveloped areas is given its sense of urgency by the material misery of these countries. Two-thirds of the world's population exist on a level so low Americans cannot even imagine it. The picture is a composite of starvation, disease, infant deaths, and short life spans on a gigantic scale, and in view of the population explosion that aggravates this misery, there are no easy solutions. There is one significant change: The world has today become a single political community. The various countries, industrial or preindustrial, no longer can lead a separate existence but become more and more aware of each other. Americans and Western Europeans, with their high standard of life, have become fellow citizens in this world community with starving Indians, disease-ridden Africans, and belabored South Americans, who therefore assume the character of underprivileged classes. Individuals in these classes may be illiterate and ignorant, and uninterested in sweeping political changes, but their leaders and manipulators are well aware of the unbelievable gap between the wealthy and the poor in this world community.

The solution most of these leaders advocate is westernization, that is, the adoption of the Western industrial way of life, the building of industries and cities, the training of the population for life and work in this environment, and the willingness to learn from Western experience in government and administration. Westernization, as advocated by revolutionary leaders in underdeveloped countries, must be seen as an act of revolt both against the old way of life and its representatives in the old ruling classes and cliques and against the West itself, for westernization is not only designed to modernize undeveloped countries and promote economic growth; it is also seen as a means of liberation and emancipation.

But what has all this to do with the development of communism? We should not be so foolish as to characterize it offhandedly as a communist conspiracy. On the contrary, some of these revolutions would have happened earlier or been more successful had Moscow been more encouraging and cooperative, or more intelligent in its leadership. Indeed, in the eyes of many Asian or African leaders, communist countries have as much potential as exploiters and oppressors as the former colonial masters or imperialist bosses. In various parts of the Third World, Marxism is regarded as but another form of ideological imperialism. Despite these reservations, communist nations may be desirable as partners in economic construction for newly established regimes. Further, Soviet, Chinese, and Cuban experiences are studied by many revolutionary leaders in underdeveloped areas and may exert a strong influence on them. In their eyes these countries appear as the first underdeveloped nations to emancipate themselves from Western influence and to succeed, at least in part, in overcoming their economic "backwardness."

When growth rates in the communist world are contrasted with the business cycle in free-enterprise societies, or with growth rates in India, Ghana, or other countries on a comparative level of development, the Soviet Union and China may become models for development, models that are the more meaningful because ideals of democracy, individual freedom, and due process are not deeply rooted in many former colonial areas, especially where colonial administrations have mocked them for decades, or these ideals may be considered luxuries less developed countries feel they cannot afford. Instead, the avowed elitism of the communist movement may appeal to revolutionary leaders in hierarchically ruled countries. In addition, communist theory has features that make it well suited to inspire such leaders. It is a sweeping theory of salvation and damnation likely to make converts in violently disturbed societies and in times of dramatic revolutionary upheavals. It is at least overtly an optimistic theory, which asserts that progress is possible—again something which seems almost deliberately designed to appeal to nations emerging from preindustrialism. Moreover, in advocating the machine age, although rebelling against Western capitalism, communist thought very precisely expresses the ambivalent attitude toward the West of people who wish to westernize even while ridding themselves of Western rule. Finally, and perhaps most significantly, communist theory, in its ideas about imperialism, incorporates a systematic theory of underdevelopment, and it is the first and perhaps even the only theory that has attempted to describe systematically the genesis and problems of underdevelopment. The communists thereby have established a virtual monopoly on explaining the underdeveloped nations to themselves; hence the curious and slightly disturbing phenomenon that spokespersons of such nations, however violently anticommunist they be, almost inevitably use the language of Lenin when they begin to talk about the economic problems of their countries. In this fashion, then, the disintegration of Western influence is at least indirectly related to the growth of communist strength since World War II.

Third World Marxism originated in Asia in the early 1920s and gradually spread to Africa, Latin America, and other areas still fighting off the traces of recent colonialism, such as the Caribbean islands and Northern Ireland. Its theoretical base is the Leninist theory of imperialism, which recognizes the existence of exploited nations kept dependent by the imperialist powers, and which regards these nations as potential auxiliary forces to the proletariat in the more industrial countries. Since the colonial powers, according to this theory, depend on cheap raw materials and labor from the underdeveloped countries, any revolt against imperialism would weaken capitalism and was therefore to be welcomed, regardless of the classes it mobilized or the ideology with which it justified this revolt. Incidentally, promoting colonial unrest or resistance to Western control anywhere would also protect the interests of the Soviet Union against the threat of being encircled and overcome by hostile capitalist countries, if only by keeping these capitalist countries preoccupied with alleviating colonial unrest.

In supporting anti-imperialist movements in the Third World, Lenin was indifferent to their ideology, partly because Marxism in China, Iran, or Arabia appeared to him premature, since these were countries virtually without modern industry and an industrial proletariat. Consequently, he allied Soviet Russia with the China of Sun Yat-sen, Turkey ruled by Kemal Atatürk, Reza Pahlevi's Iran, and Ibn Saud in Arabia; he also seems to have been sympathetic toward the Congress party in India. In these policies he was often at odds with the small communist parties or groups that formed throughout the areas we now call the Third World. Such parties or groups were typically led by Western-educated people for whom the Russian Revolution represented the first successful attempt of an underdeveloped country to shake off the yoke of imperialism and who now looked to Moscow for support in their attempt to emancipate their own country. Third World communism from the very beginning was linked to struggles for national liberation.

Support was not always forthcoming. In Moscow and throughout the world of communist parties, bitter disputes raged over the question of whether supporting communist movements in countries without a sizable proletariat made any sense, or if such a movement did exist, what policies or strategies it should be advised to pursue. Analogous disputes raged within the budding communist movements in the Third World, and some of the principal questions raised in the 1920s have never been fully resolved. Nonetheless, some general patterns for communist revolutions in the Third World have emerged from these disputes, even though actual practices have varied from one country and one period to another. To summarize the general trends manifested in Third World Marxism, the strategies pursued by the Chinese Communist party in its struggle for power will serve as a model.

China was one of the oldest civilizations. Vast in size and population, it had a culture, a system of government, and a complex belief system that were more than two thousand years old. In the eyes of Western observers two hundred years ago, old China was a model of stability and wise rule. However, the culture has been profoundly disturbed by Western encroachments ever since the early nineteenth century and since then has been racked by dissent and revolution, tyranny and anarchy. More and more the country became the prey of profit- and power-hungry industrial nations. Meanwhile, in the ensuing turmoil, Chinese intellectuals turned to Western ideas such as Christianity, liberalism, and socialism to orient themselves.

Communism arose in China as a reaction to the humiliations some Chinese felt China received in the peace negotiations following World War I, where Western domination over the country was, in effect, reaffirmed. By accepting revolutionary Marxism, which came to them in its Bolshevik form, Chinese intellectuals could repudiate their own culture, which they considered outmoded and exploitative, while at the same time rejecting Western capitalism and imperialism.

China in the 1920s was still primarily a country of landlords and peasants, bureaucrats and soldiers, merchants and artisans. Industry, in the modern sense of the word, was concentrated in a few cities, which were virtual outposts of European civilization. Capitalism was a foreign importation that had made only superficial dents on the surface of Chinese society. The small industrial proletariat was hardly a factor in Chinese politics. For a Marxist, who seeks to promote the proletarian revolution, all this implies difficult problems of strategy and timing.

Throughout the 1920s, the small and inexperienced Chinese Communist party was dominated by the Communist International, the world-wide organization of communist parties that had its headquarters in Moscow. It was virtually run by Russian communists and in its policies was closely attuned to the perceptions and preferences of the people who were governing the

Soviet Union. The policies which these people dictated to their Chinese comrades turned out to be disastrous failures which nearly destroyed the Chinese communist movement. However, in the mid-1930s a group of leaders under Mao Zedong (Mao Tsetung) took command over the remnants of the movement and initiated the strategy that fifteen years later resulted in their assuming power over all of China. Mao's strategies contained some startling innovations, which have become characteristic features of Third World communism.

While Marxism in its original form declared the industrial proletariat to be the only class that could emancipate all humanity from exploitation and domination, Mao's doctrine recognized the peasantry as the great mass of the oppressed and hence as the class that must be mobilized for revolution. His strategy therefore focused on the countryside, not the city. Some adherents of Mao's strategy, in China and elsewhere, have gone so far as to write off the industrial proletariat altogether. Thus Regis Debray, a French communist inspired by the Cuban revolution more than by the Chinese one, declared in his book, *Revolution within the Revolution*, that anyone who had grown up in a city was by that very fact rendered unable to be a genuine revolutionary. The Chinese party was successful in establishing itself in some remote areas of rural China, where it instituted land reforms and began to teach the peasants self-reliance, so that they might forget centuries of subservience, stand up against their landlords, and learn to govern themselves. Unlike Lenin, who was convinced that the masses of the exploited would have to be led by an enlightened elite, Mao urged the communist leadership to pay much closer attention to the opinions and experiences of the people at the bottom of society. He also took great pains in translating the ideology of the party into language and imagery that Chinese peasants could understand. This concern over continual exchange of views and experiences between the political leadership and the people at the grass roots has come to be known as the "mass line."

· In the areas under their control, the Chinese communists wooed the peasantry by land reform and built an ever-growing army which was skillfully led and seems to have fought with considerable enthusiasm. By and large they seem to have been successful also in doing away with one of the root evils of traditional

China—corruption. This may have been an important factor in gaining the support of vast numbers of people. Gradually, they expanded the areas under their control, and the strength and skill of their troops grew, especially as a result of the many years of fighting the Japanese, who had begun to invade China in 1931. This participation of communist armies in the anti-Japanese resistance may in the end have been the most important factor in making communist rule an acceptable alternative to the corrupt and inefficient dictatorship of the Guomindang under General Jiang Kaishek (Chiang Kai-shek).

Chinese communist revolutionary strategy thus yields a pattern quite different from that of the Russian Revolution: It focuses on the countryside and establishes its hold over "liberated areas" through land reform and "clean" government. In the protracted civil war, which in China *preceded* the revolutionary takeover, the cities were last; in the Russian Revolution they had come first. Chinese communism emphasized the need for forging strong links with the masses and making communications between leaders and followers a genuine two-way process. Finally, the party buttressed its legitimacy by claiming to represent the interests of the nation, rather than those of dominant foreign powers, whereas in the Russian Revolution the claims of Russian national interests had at first been repudiated.

With many variations, this has been the pattern for communist revolutions also in Southeast Asia, Africa, Cuba, and Central America. The variations are a matter of controversy, and so is the basic pattern, especially since it is contrary to some of the basic assumptions made by Engels and Marx. These two founders of communism believed that communism would first come in the most advanced countries, not in the underdeveloped ones; that the proletariat, and not the peasantry, would make the revolution; and that it would make sense for them to do so only after capitalism had accumulated the material preconditions for communism—a modern industrial base.

Once in control of the vast Chinese subcontinent, the government of the newly established People's Republic of China quickly organized itself on lines similar to the Soviet state and instituted sweeping social changes designed to weaken or destroy big capitalism, both domestic and foreign, and landlord control. By these measures the regime tried to attract mass support among workers, peasants, and intellectuals, establish firm control over the economy, destroy hostile classes, emancipate the economy from foreign control and ownership, and rehabilitate a productive system gutted by years of occupation and war.

At the same time, some of the methods of the Chinese Communist party were quite different from those applied in Russia. The chief difference at first was the party's attempt to collaborate with elements of the former ruling classes, thus to mitigate class warfare and to eradicate capitalism by nonviolent methods. In order to rationalize these differences, Chinese communists had to redefine the concept of the dictatorship of the proletariat and the idea of the best road toward socialism. These unorthodox innovations were tolerated even by Stalin.

By 1953 the government of Mao Zedong was sufficiently confident to lauch its First Five-Year Plan, which was to carry the economic transformation of the country a significant step further. While the first years of communist rule had eliminated landlords and absentee capitalists, the First Five-Year Plan was to prepare the way for the collectivization of agriculture and the total socialization of industry and handicraft. China thus tried to copy the rapid transformations undergone by the Soviet economy, but in far less time, even though the base from which China started was infinitely more backward that the Russia economy of 1917. The Chinese leaders claimed that this faster rate of revolutionary transformation was made possible by generous Soviet aid and by the more advanced state of modern technology. By the fall of 1956, the outlines of the Second Five-Year Plan began to take shape. It was formally adopted in early 1957 and began to be implemented in 1958. Its goal was to drive the Chinese economy and society into the "Great Leap Forward" to industrialism and socialism. Production goals were set that seemed fantastically high to Western economists, and some did in fact prove to be unrealistic. Methods of organization and management were applied that in centralization and unyielding collectivism outstripped anything that had been undertaken by Soviet society. The Mao regime even claimed that China might virtually skip some of the stages of development that had marked the history of the USSR. The most spectacular of these social experiments was the transformation of agriculture from an individual peasant system to a thoroughly collective system and the concomitant merger of agricultural pursuit with industrial construction. Unlike the Soviet *kolkhoz*, the Chinese commune makes not the slightest concessions to individualism or to family traditions. Instead, it is an attempt to apply the organizational form of the labor gang or the drill platoon not only to farming operations, large-scale construction work, and other primary economic pursuits but also to all possible human activities, including housing, feeding, education, and recreation. Here was the utter militarization of life in the intensity demanded for the working class in Plato's utopia. Vast masses of people organized into disciplined labor armies were deployed in building dams and other waterworks, roads, railroads, and entire industrial enterprises, so that the Chinese people seem to be building much of their new industrial base in bucket-brigade fashion, with legions of unskilled manual labor. These people's communes were to combine all administrative and economic functions, and the party therefore claimed that they were leading directly to the withering away of the state. More generally, Mao and his comrades asserted that the Great Leap Forward and the establishment of people's communes should be regarded as a direct step into communism, and one implication was that China might reach that happy stage before the USSR.

The Great Leap Forward, however, turned into a dismal failure; and it was followed by a period of retrenchment and caution. The leadership of the party even encouraged criticism and dissent. "Let a hundred flowers bloom and a hundred thoughts contend," wrote Mao. However, he and his associates were then obviously perturbed by the ardor and the variety of dissatisfaction which came to the fore, and they curbed the newly encouraged freedom of expressing dissent very quickly. The problems facing the Chinese leadership were seriously aggravated by the sudden rupture of relations with the Soviet Union, which meant that no more material assistance could be expected from Moscow or any of its allies in Eastern Europe. The break itself was the result of deep hostilities between Russia and China, which had been building up for centuries preceding the communist revolutions and had been exacerbated by misunderstandings and failings in the relations between the two communist parties.

Partly as a result of this rupture, the Chinese leadership repeatedly stressed its own contributions to communist practice and its criticism of the Soviet pattern. How might one summarize the difference between them? In their simplest form, Mao's method of transforming a nation into a communist one suggests that socialism cannot be built on the basis of industrial development alone but must also develop in the minds of the people, or perhaps that it must *first* develop in people's minds. That consciousness, not material means of production, is the rock on which socialism must be founded. Once this is said, education or reeducation turns out to be as important as production, and in its most radical form, this may turn into the belief that socialism and communism can be established without modern technology. Hence Mao's experiments with the use of ''barefoot doctors,'' with folk medicine, and with blast furnaces in every farm yard.

In China under Mao such ideas may have been a case of making virtue out of necessity. But Mao's special brand of folk communism was the result not only of his resentment against the Russians and his isolation from the world; it seems clear that he also feared the prospect of bureaucratization and what it might do to the revolutionary élan of the movement. Similarly, he seems to have feared or resented technically and scientifically trained specialists, either because he considered them imbued with anti-revolutionary tendencies or because he thought of them as representatives of the imperialist West.

To prevent these dangers, Mao at times deliberately mobilized the masses of peasants, workers, or soldiers against the new elites that the victorious revolution had installed. Or to put it slightly differently, he seems on occasions to have made deliberate attempts to upset the newly established communist order by encouraging disorder and chaos. He argued that revolution, in order to be successful, must continually renew itself, just as Thomas Jefferson once argued that the tree of liberty must be watered with the blood of revolutionary martyrs again and again if it is to stay alive.

The most important and spectacular development of this kind was the so-called Cultural Revolution which Mao and his associates unleashed in the late 1960s. Claiming that the country was in danger of abandoning its revolutionary ideals, Mao mobilized the broad masses of the poor and the young against all authorities, the party, the government bureaucracy, and all people of learning—experts, scholars, and intellectuals. He encouraged them to proclaim their faith in the total equality of all, including the right of the masses to take all public life into their own collective hands. As a result, countless institutions of government, education, and other public affairs were closed, their cadres sent to labor camps or to farm communes where they were ordered to haul garbage, clean latrines, or in other ways humiliate themselves and atone for their former privileged positions. The effect of this attempt to renew the revolutionary spirit seems to have been disastrous.

Both the Great Leap Forward and the Cultural Revolution may have been part of Mao's effort to dissociate himself and his country from the post-Stalinist leadership of the Soviet Union, whom he denounced as Revisionists and as traitors to the cause of communism—an opinion which the Soviet leaders, in their turn, voiced about him. Ever since Khrushchev broke relations with the Chinese communist regime, Moscow and Peking have denounced each other and regarded each other as major threats to security. This deep antagonism is based not only on an antagonism between Russia and China which goes back many centuries, but has more immediate roots: in the shabby treatment which the Chinese Communist party received from the Comintern in the 1920s and 1930s, in the fundamental differences between Leninist and Maoist revolutionary strategies, and in Mao's deep fear of the bureaucratization of the revolution. But such a process of bureaucratization, in his opinion, had already taken place in the Soviet Union.

One major sequel to the disaster which the Cultural Revolution wrought was the decision of the Chinese regime to come to terms with the United States, a country against which it had fought a bloody war in Korea. Now Washington and Peking resumed relations. The People's Republic of China was seated in the United Nations, replacing the Republic of China (i.e., the government of Taiwan) as a permanent member of the UN Security Council; and thus a second communist country was welcomed into the ranks of the most important world powers.

There is, incidentally, one additional reason which may have contributed to the break between the Soviet Union and China. After Stalin's death, Mao may have believed in all sincerity that he would now be recognized as the "Number One" communist in the world, since he had credentials as the leader of a successful revolution which nobody in the Soviet Union could have matched. His colleagues in the USSR and in Eastern Europe, however, had not the slightest inclination to proclaim him as the leader of global communism. Moreover, while the Chinese regime continued to pay homage to the memory of Stalin, his successors in Moscow proceeded to revile that memory. It is ironic to note that since his own death Mao has shared Stalin's fate. His successors, too, have begun to denounce him and reverse his policies. Mao's death has led to a juggling for position in the Chinese party which is still going on as this is being written. The most spectacular event in this connection was the arrest, trial, and conviction of the most radical Maoists, headed by Mao's widow. This was the so-called Gang of Four.

The contemporary leadership of the Chinese People's Republic appears eager to steer the country into a much more moderate course, to adopt Western technologies and Western organization, to raise living standards, and to replace a policy of permanent revolution with some sort of administrative stability. Their country is still desperately poor. Its population is growing at a rate which its rulers view with great alarm. Controversies within the party over the measures to cope with these and many other pressing problems must be very sharp; and the further development of the Chinese revolution will be exceedingly interesting to watch.

THE CUBAN REVOLUTION

Cuba had been a Spanish colony since the days of Columbus. Its economy, until the early nineteenth century, was a plantation economy based on slavery, the system which prevailed all around the Caribbean basin. The nineteenth century saw a great deal of peasant unrest and the rise of revolutionary nationalism and revolutionary liberalism, erupting into actual revolutionary movements in the 1860s. As a result of the Spanish-American war, Cuba gained independence, only to become economically and politically dependent on its big neighbor to the north, the United States. Through most of the 1940s and 1950s, the country was governed by a military man, Fulgencio Batista, who at first ruled in the spirit of liberal reformism, but later turned into a corrupt and arbitrary dictator. Various opposition movements tried to organize against him, and a young lawyer named Fidel Castro took a leading role in an abortive uprising by liberal students. He was apprehended, tried, and convicted, but granted amnesty after spending some time in jail. In the mid-fifties, Castro and a small band of revolutionaries established themselves in the mountain wilderness of eastern Cuba and began to organize the local peasants for revolution, using tactics similar to those of the Chinese communists. Within a few years the revolt had spread, and on New Year's Day 1960 the Batista government collapsed. Castro and his *rebeldes* (rebels) rode into Havana and began to rule the country.

This did not at first seem to be a victory for communism. In fact, the Cuban communists had supported Batista and had thrown their support to Castro only very shortly before his victory: They had denounced his tactics as un-Marxist. Moreover, once he was in power, he treated the Cuban communists with a good deal of contempt, accepting the collaboration of some but jailing many others. He seems to have believed that even a resolutely independent left-wing Cuban regime could maintain good relations with the United States. However, the Kennedy administration rebuffed him and sought to keep him under control by punitive trade policies. Castro then turned to the communist world for allies, declared that he had been a Marxist all his life, and re-shaped the Cuban economy and state on the neo-Stalinist model. The results, so far, are mixed, partly because of the difficulties placed in Cuba's path by the United States, and partly because of costly mistakes made by the Castro regime. The country still is very poor, though one must view this within the perspective of neighboring countries in the Caribbean area, which are, if anything, less well off. Moreover, in Cuba the poverty is shared much more equally than it was a generation ago. Serious efforts have been made to raise the level of education and training for wide strata of the population (for whom this had not been available) and to train people for cooperation and mutual respect, to mobilize women for wage work and for participation in public life, and in general to lay the foundation for socialist human relations. At the same time the regime appears to have become as bureaucratized as other communist regimes, and it continues to impose central control over all associations and ideas as relentlessly as analogous regimes in Europe and Asia.

Moreover, the Cuban government made repeated attempts to spread its revolution to other parts of Latin America and the Caribbean area. In recent years, Cuba "volunteers" have also served in various areas of Africa, where socialist or communist movements of national liberation fought against more conservative rivals or against the old colonial powers.

THE NATURE OF THIRD WORLD COMMUNISM

Regimes of a communist type now exist in large numbers in Africa, Asia, Central America, and in the Caribbean. These are countries whose political leaders identify with Marxist-Leninist doctrines and cultivate close ties with one or several of the major communist powers. They have come into power either because the former colonial powers withdrew or as a result of lengthy and bitter war both against the former colonial nations and against competing domestic parties or factions. This is not a unified group, and its composition remains unstable. Moreover, it often is difficult to distinguish Marxist-Leninist regimes from those not so labeled. All Third World regimes face similar problems, and the range of options they have for solving them is limited. At times it seems as if the ideological labels and forms or organization are little more than symbols of national self-assertion against the Western world.

Indeed, it could be argued that the fundamental conflicts between the West and the Third World are not so much over differing ideologies, such as democracy, capitalism, Marxism, or communism, but are rather a centuries-old quest for *control* and management of natural resources, land, and people. However, the debate over ideology, dominance, and imperialism will continue. While the Third World was once considered politically unimportant and ignored (except for the extraction of resources), the Third World is now an essential and volatile element in the world political arena. By studying historical revolutions and regimes, it is possible to trace the development of nation-states and ideologies and perhaps gain insights into future changes.

CHAPTER 11

Reform Communism in Europe and North America

World War II not only set in motion the world-wide rebellion against European colonialism, it also significantly changed the map and the political configuration of Europe itself. Of all the changes, the most profound one was the division of Europe into two parts: Western Europe under liberal constitutional regimes affiliated with the Atlantic alliance, and Eastern Europe under regimes modeled after the USSR and allied with the Soviet Union, with a few states trying to steer clear of close attachment to either of these blocs. In this chapter we will survey the development of communism in both groups of European states.

The Soviet advance into Eastern Europe began in September 1939 when, on the basis of its recent agreement with the Third Reich, the USSR annexed the eastern half of Poland. Supported by the same treaty, it added the three Baltic republics as well as parts of Finland and Rumania in the following year. All these territories were lost again to the Germans in 1941, but Moscow kept claiming a legal right to them, and her new allies in the West did not consider it opportune to challenge these claims openly. Moreover, the wartime governments of Britain and the United States considered themselves so dependent on continued Soviet cooperation that in their agreements with Stalin they conceded to him overriding influence in all of Eastern Europe except Greece. Provisions guaranteeing the independence and democratic nature of the postwar regimes to be set up in Eastern Europe were left deliberately vague. In effect, therefore, the Western powers allotted or sold these countries to the Russians; they thought at the time that such a deal was inevitable.

If Stalin was thus given a fairly free hand in transforming Eastern Europe according to the Soviet image, the local communist parties were aided by a number of additional circumstances. Their record in the resistance movements gave them some prestige and a claim to a share in power. The old ruling classes had been decimated by the occupation or stigmatized as collaborationists; their parties had dwindled or were outlawed; their property had been taken over by the Germans and, after liberation, was often retained by the new governments as being enemy property. Many people in Balkanized Eastern Europe, moreover, were weary of bloody conflict between national minorities, and some of them may have been impressed with the Soviet solution of this problem. In some of the Eastern European countries age-old feelings of kinship with the Russians had been reawakened and could be exploited by the communists. It may also be that the memory of the Munich pact, by which England and France delivered the Czechoslovak Republic to Hitler in 1938, served to discredit the Western nations among many people in Eastern Europe. Thus, in spite of widespread hatred or fear of the Russians or of communism, many factors predisposed many people in this area to accept socialism and collaborate with the communists. Nonetheless, the transformation of Eastern Europe into a set of purely communist regimes had to be done by a combination of stealth and force, utilizing all the advantages the communists possessed by virtue of the Soviet army's presence. The transformation was, on the whole, well managed and was accomplished in less than four years. By the spring of 1948 all governments in Eastern Europe were in essence communist dictatorships. Although formally these regimes were governed by parties with a broader following and a more diffuse ideology than communist parties, for practical purposes these coalition parties were full-fledged communist parties. By means of thorough purges and other less bloody maneuvers, Stalin managed to place every one of these parties under the command of people absolutely loyal and obedient to him, little Stalins themselves, who faithfully followed every cue Moscow gave them and ruthlessly enforced their commands through means of government tested in the USSR. Party dictatorship, police terror, forced collectivization, economic centralization, consumer austerity, and the strictest control of all human activities came to characterize the regimes of Eastern Europe, while, in turn, Moscow maintained its own control over them by a variety of methods. In the ten years following the end of World War II, communist government in Eastern Europe resulted in rapid industrial growth and equally rapid social dislocation—a scrambling of society that, in the short run, gave rise to tremendous tensions and dissatisfactions, especially among the urban workers and intellectuals, but which, in the long run, was doubtless designed to make communist government more acceptable to these nations. The undeniable success of the regimes in transforming their countries in the Soviet image and raising them to the level of industrial nations was marred, however, by several factors: Soviet economic exploitation robbed them of much of the fruits of their labor and, in fact, may have retarded industrial development; economic growth was perverted by strong strivings for autarky, which were encouraged by the Kremlin, although they may also have been the result of the surprising amount of national antagonism between the various Eastern European regimes. Perhaps the most serious criticism that can be leveled against the Soviet policy of imposing its pattern of government and management on the nations of Eastern Europe is that this uniformity was bound to be counterproductive politically and economically. The Soviet style of government has grown out of the soil of Russian political culture, hence by definition is foreign to the political traditions and experiences of Poland, Hungary, or Czechoslovakia. The command economy set up by Stalin may have been very effective in transforming a peasant nation like Russia into an industrial empire, but in countries that were already well on their way to industrialization or that, like Czechoslovakia, had attained the level of the most modern countries, it could only wreak damage. In short, these regimes were artificial creations, not intended to conform to the hopes of the native communist leadership. They were set up by the Soviet occupation authorities for purely Soviet purposes. Their establishment increased tne military, political, and economic strength of the Soviet Union, and if the interests of the Soviet Union are identified with those of world communism as a whole, then the entire communist world was strengthened. From the point of view of the countries transformed, the establishment of these client regimes undoubtedly was deplorable: If these were revolutions, they were revolutions gone astray, skewed in their development by outside interference. And, because such imposed regimes, whatever their achievements, cannot ever govern benignly, the Sovietization of Eastern Europe, on the whole, served to discredit the communist cause in the eyes of the world.

Among the communist leaders who acquired power in Eastern Europe after the war were many who, despite their devotion to the movement and to Soviet Russia as its center, were hopeful that some of the harshest features of the Soviet way of life might be avoided in their own countries. The low living standard and the unyielding dictatorship of the communist bosses, the reign of the police and the general disregard for the happiness of individuals and groups, the lack of intellectual freedom and the hermetic isolation of Soviet citizens from the outside world—these and other features were explained as necessary consequences of Russia's underdeveloped state or of Russian political traditions. In countries like Czechoslovakia, Poland, Hungary, and East Germany, where an industrial base already existed, where the old ruling class had been wiped out or discredited, where liberal traditions were well ingrained, and where socialism was generally accepted as inevitable if not desirable, many native communists sincerely believed that something like a democratic or at least more humane type of communism could be developed and that the Soviet pattern of development need not necessarily be followed in all its details. In short, the Kremlin's effort to force the Eastern European regimes to adopt Stalinist methods of "building socialism" came into conflict with the obvious fact that the nations of that area lived under circumstances differing from those in the USSR. They lived by different intellectual traditions and on different levels of economic and social development. These differences were acknowledged, at least temporarily, even by the Kremlin high command and found reflection in various doctrinal adjustments. For instance, the communist regimes of Eastern Europe were not designated as soviet republics; moreover, the fact that the countries of Eastern Europe were not incorporated in the Soviet Union was an explicit concession to the strength of nationalism in that area. Despite such doctrinal adjustments, however, the actual governing of the Eastern European countries was more similar to the Soviet pattern than was acceptable to many of their political leaders, including some communists.

It is ironic that the man who became the spokesman for such protest views was the one Eastern European leader who harbored the greatest reservations about them. Marshal Tito, the ruler of Yugoslavia, was the most loyal Stalinist of all the postwar leaders of Eastern Europe and the least sympathetic to the "revisionist" views of some of his colleagues in neighboring countries. Circumstances, however, caused him to quarrel with his colleagues in Moscow, and when he stood his ground, he unexpectedly found himself labeled a heretic and an outcast from the communist fold, a traitor to the revolution and an agent of imperialism. Once in this position, he was bound, though only very gradually and cautiously, to justify his status ideologically. Consequently, his regime began to express systematically some of the disappointed hopes of Eastern European communists. Moreover, many communists in Western countries seem to have been inspired by the notion of communism without some of the most obnoxious features of Soviet rule—an autonomous, polycentric, humane, perhaps even democratic communism. The stirrings in Eastern Europe and the successful resistance to Moscow of Tito were thus echoed by lively debates and a good deal of soul searching among communists and their sympathizers in Western Europe and North America, who now envisaged a non-Russian alternative to Stalinism.

In Eastern Europe, the yearning for more moderate methods was without doubt based primarily on an awareness of the sharp tensions and dissatisfactions created by communist policies. The aim of the "revisionists" was to ease the tensions and alleviate the dissatisfaction. Very likely the tougher-minded "Stalinists" who won over them temporarily were just as much aware of the underlying difficulties. But instead of giving way to popular sentiment, they doubtless hoped to overcome these difficulties by suppressing them and thus all the more rapidly transforming society in the communist image. In other words, they were intent on allaying dissatisfaction and unrest through industrialization and collectivization. Eastern European communism thus found itself engaged in the same great debate that shook the Russian

Communist party during the period of the New Economic Policy.

This time, the conflict was solved, for the time being, with the help of the Kremlin. While it may have seemed implausible at the time to assume that Eastern European revisionist ideas consti- tuted a threat to the Soviet Union, Stalin took vigorous action to suppress all such notions. He may have had any or all of the following reasons for his intolerance. He may have realized more clearly than Western observers that these ideas could produce open rebellions such as those which occurred in Germany, Czechoslovakia, Poland, and Hungary in 1953 and 1956. He may also have worried about the impact the development of some sort of democratic communism anywhere might have had on his own Russian population: If the Poles and the Czechs had been granted more freedom and a higher standard of living, the Soviet people might have demanded the same. In addition, distrust of autonomy and the urge to control and coordinate is endemic in the communist system of government. It so happened, moreover, that unorthodox ideas of this kind were particularly popular among communists who had fought in resistance movements in their own countries or who had spent the war years in exile in the West. The Russians, apparently, did not trust such communists and sought to replace them with faithful organization people who had spent the war years and perhaps more in the Soviet Union, who may even have weathered the great purges of the 1930s and were known as loyal and safe. The principal reason, however, which compelled Stalin to suppress the revisionists was the fact that he did not care to permit the people of Poland, Czechoslovakia, and other countries possessing an in- dustrial base to benefit from this higher economic development. Instead, he wanted to divert a maximal share of the products of these countries to the USSR, for the sake of reconstructing his own ravaged country and raising the living standard of his own population. This policy implied the drastic imposition of an austerity regime in the Eastern European satellites, together with pressures for harsh work discipline and totalitarian conformity, dashing the hopes for autonomy and democratic communism.

In short, not only were the "revolutions" which brought com- munism to Eastern Europe contrived by outside intervention, but they also did not establish regimes that were able to bring about social reforms appropriate for these countries. Nevertheless, heretical beliefs and hopes never did perish among the communists of Eastern Europe. And in subsequent years, their heresy was to present the Soviet Union with grave political problems. These problems came into the open after Stalin's death.

Stalin's death in March 1953 brought with it a slight relaxation of tension. The "breaking of the ice" (usually translated as the "thaw") noted by Soviet intellectuals made itself felt also in international affairs: While still stressing the basic incompatibility between capitalist and communist goals and methods, the leaders of the communist world gave new stress to the themes of peaceful coexistence, constructive competition, and an easing of tensions. Within the communist camp, Moscow showed some toleration of revisionist or autonomist heresies in Eastern Europe; in these countries, too, doctrinal discipline was relaxed somewhat, and the Eastern European regimes were allowed to experiment with administrative or economic methods hitherto prohibited. The emergence of a communist China had already made it necessary for Moscow to make allowances for differences in method and ideology, if only by implication, for with Mao Zedong and Zhou Enlai (Chou En-lai) men had come to power who were the equals, not the subordinates or creatures, of the rulers in Moscow. By 1955 Moscow had extended the principle that socialist development may take different forms to Yugoslavia. The dissolution of the already moribund Cominform in 1956 was merely a symbol of this rapprochement between Moscow and Belgrade. Furthermore, Khrushchev's speech at the Twentieth Congress of the Soviet Communist Party, in which he denounced Stalin, served as a major stimulus for opening the floodgates of criticism in all communist parties, including those of Eastern Europe.

Students of revolution have often observed that in any society where the existing system is hated or held in contempt, and where it is kept together only with the help of tight controls, a relaxation of controls will not bring about contentment and acceptance but will instead release pent-up resentment. Where the spirit of resistance smolders underneath the surface, conciliatory steps may cause the fire to flare up instead of smothering it. This is what has happened in Eastern Europe in the three decades since Stalin's death.

Dissent, dissatisfaction, deviation from orthodoxy, reform movements, and outright rebellion have come to Eastern Europe in various forms. The following brief survey can do no more than suggest the variety of these forms.

In Yugoslavia, communism went its own way after it became clear to Tito that the breach with Moscow could not be healed and that Stalinist methods of government led to disastrous results. Under his leadership, the Yugoslav communists have experimented with various institutions designed to decentralize authority, allow for greater citizen participation, and redefine the role of the communist party. In world affairs Yugoslavia has sought to remain free from alignment with either the communist or the Western powers. It has cultivated trade relations with both blocs, opened its borders both to Western visitors and to Yugoslav citizens seeking temporary employment in Western Europe, and permitted the revival of free enterprise on a significant scale. Perhaps the most innovative experiment was the reform that gave ownership and management of all major enterprises to all the workers employed therein. This attempt to establish self-management of workers is being observed with considerable attention in the communist and noncommunist world. Any verdict on its benefits and drawbacks, on its success or failure, would be premature.

Less bold deviations from the Soviet pattern are widespread in Eastern Europe. The Rumanian regime, in many ways a faithful replica of the Soviet model, nonetheless is pursuing a somewhat indepedent foreign policy. The Hungarian government in 1956 was on the verge of losing control when a reform movement that had begun within the party leadership and among party intellectuals turned into a popular revolution against communism and Soviet domination. The regime was "rescued" by Soviet troops which marched in, suppressed the revolution, killed some of the leading reform communists, and installed a leader who seemed willing to be loyal to Moscow. But after some years of cautious maneuvering, the Hungarian regime under this same leader, Janos Kádár, has instituted fairly bold economic reforms which incorporate the decentralization of management and limited free enterprise; it has increased trade relations with the West and allowed some loosening of controls over ideas. On the whole, the effects of these reforms seem to have been beneficial: Living standards have risen, efficiency has been increased, and the population seems readier to accept the system.

A close look at developments in Eastern Europe will show that similar statements can be made about virtually every country in that group. The party leadership has experimented everywhere with organizational forms, patterns of management, or social policies that deviated from the models established in the USSR. In every case this was done in response to problems specific to the country or in conformity with national traditions. While in some cases the reforms were successful, in other important cases the problems were not solved and sometimes were even aggravated.

One example of such failure is the case of Czechoslovakia. Economically and politically on a par with Western Europe, the country had come through World War II with minimal damage to its social fabric and its economic base. Yet once it came under exclusive communist rule, the Stalinist pattern of planning and management was imposed on the Czechs, as if they were still in the stage of primitive accumulation. As a result, the once-flourishing industrial economy became inefficient and lost its ability to compete in the world market. As the deterioration became more and more obvious, some of the leading economists in the party began to advocate reforms in economic planning and management, which in turn set off more general discussions within the party about the need for a wider variety of reforms: the democratization of the whole system, the lifting of censorship, more meaningful participation, the punishment of police and party officials responsible for arbitrary actions, especially the bloody show trials of some party leaders that had been staged in the early 1950s, and similar changes. The Czech Communist party responded to these demands with fairly sweeping personnel changes and reforms. In early 1968, the Czechoslovak Socialist Republic seemed well on the way toward transforming itself into a more liberal and more democratic communist system. But the reforms contemplated went further than the Soviet leadership believed it could tolerate; and, after giving repeated warning to the Czechoslovak leadership, Soviet troops and units from other Warsaw Pact countries marched in, deposed the reformist leaders, and restored the authority of those who had resisted the reform movement. Thus, the so-called Prague Spring of 1968 was of short duration.

The most serious challenges to the East European communist regimes have come in two forms: working-class rebellion and Marxist critiques of Stalinist and neo-Stalinist practices. They are the most serious challenges because communist regimes claim to be following Marxist doctrine and indeed to be the guardians of Marxist orthodoxy. They also claim to be representing the interests of the working class and tend to take the loyalty of the workers for granted. Yet workers have repeatedly repudiated these regimes, and theoreticians from within the Marxist movement have used Marxist arguments to assert that these systems deviate from communist ideology. When these two challenges join forces, as they seem to have done in Poland between 1980 and 1982, communist systems are in deep trouble.

Apart from the 1953 workers' uprisings in the German Democratic Republic and in Czechoslovakia, workers' protest against communist rule has taken its most serious form and occurred most often in Poland. To explain this adequately would require a discussion of Polish geography, history, and national culture too detailed for this book. Let it simply be said that, for very complex reasons, the Polish people, including the working class, have shown themselves most resistant to communist rule. The Polish party has consistently been the most incapable of making the system work, and the superpower on its Eastern border, that is, the USSR, has also been unable to keep these problems under control. As this book is being revised, martial law in Poland, in force for twelve months, has just been lifted. The Polish economy is still in terrible shape, scarcities still plague the population, and the people have not made their peace with the regime. None of the major problems that led to the crisis has been resolved. Meanwhile the leadership in neighboring communist countries can be expected to observe their own working classes with nervous apprehension, wondering whether the rebellious mood has crossed the Polish borders.

For heresies in communist theory, Eastern Europe has always been fertile soil, if only because admiration for the Russian Revolution often was mixed and in conflict with a deep commitment to Western (as opposed to Russian) intellectual and political traditions. One can observe this conflict in the writings of the influential Hungarian communist philosopher, George Lukács, whose life work can be interpreted as an attempt, however flawed, to link Lenin's revolutionary communism with the traditions of Western humanism. With Lukács, this attempt goes back to the early 1920s. In the final analysis, his work is feeble and half-hearted, but it did serve to inspire and encourage subsequent theorists within the communist parties to become sharper in their criticism of Stalinism and its application to Eastern Europe. The variety of approaches taken by the many East European communists in their attempt to provide a Marxist critique of Soviet rule is too great to be discussed here. Several major contributors to this literature have, in the end, dissociated themselves from Marxism altogether; others still confess it. Some have emigrated, others are in jail in their native country, and others still occupy party positions.

Few people have observed political and ideological developments, especially reform movements and rebellions, with greater attention than leaders and theorists of communist parties in Western Europe and other advanced industrial countries, such as Japan. The efforts of East European reform communists have much affinity with attempts made in several Western communist parties to redefine communist policies and communist theory so as to make them viable in advanced countries. In recent years, this attempt has been named Euro-Communism.

Euro-Communism and its precursor movements are based on the recognition that the cause of communism has not been advanced by the USSR. The Russian party imposed too much conformity on the world communist movement, forcing parties to adopt policies, tactics, and forms of organization that might have made sense in Russia but were foreign to Italy or Great Britain. Any party, if it wishes to be successful, must speak the language, follow the customs, and work within the institutions of the country within which it operates. As the phrase goes, every country must go its own road toward communism. This phrase, incidentally, was first coined in the 1920s by such people as N. N. Bukharin, a Soviet leader who advocated a more gradual, less cruel and painful method than Stalin's and by his supporters in other communist parties. It was taken up in the 1940s by Earl Browder, then the leader of the Communist party of the United States, who argued that it would be a mistake to apply Russian or European political strategies and organization in the United States, because America was different. His arguments were called "American exceptionalism." In contemporary Euro-Communism (i.e., the views preached by the leaders of communist parties in Spain, Italy, Japan, and the Scandinavian countries, among others), similar ideas are linked with criticism of the Soviet Union; attempts are made to mediate between the superpowers, and to forge broad alliances with parties and groups to the left of center, including the Catholic Church and other religious groups. Futhermore, Euro-Communists tend to redefine the revolution they seek by suggesting that it will not be an armed uprising but will take the form of victory at the ballot box. Euro-Communism professes a commitment to the struggle for power within the framework of the existing constitutions.

In short, the leaders of Western European reform communism (and those of some non-European communist parties, especially that of Japan) have expressed an awareness that by appearing too closely tied to the Soviet Union, its policies, and its interests, and by adhering too rigidly to strategies which may have been successful in Russia but made little sense in their own countries, they were alienating large numbers of potential adherents. Italian and French communists, moreover, have held important local and regional offices ever since the end of World War II. They have often shown themselves capable managers, free of corruption, and willing to compromise; in the eyes of some observers they have established model governments in the communities and regions under their control. In turn, this experience has moderated some of these officials and has given them a stake in the existing political system. Euro-Communism is an interpretation of Marxist-Leninist doctrine which is decidedly pragmatic. In this it has begun to resemble the orthodox Marxism preached and practiced around the turn of the century by the leaders and theoreticians of the Second International.

CHAPTER 12

Conclusion

Since the global revolution that began in earnest in 1917, communism has been one of the chief moving forces and one of the principal gainers. The main thrust of communism, however, has not been to transform capitalist societies into socialist ones. Instead, it had functioned as an agent for the promotion of industrial growth and general modernization in essentially precapitalist societies. Communism has acted as a substitute for capitalism in underdeveloped countries, and it has played this role in the name of national liberation from foreign domination. In both its fervent nationalism and its focused attention on the problems of accumulation, twentieth-century communism is very different from anything Engels or Marx had in mind.

Despite many setbacks and some serious limits to its long-range effectiveness, communism has shown itself to be a rather successful pattern of modernization, one that can stand comparison with such noncommunist success stories as Brazil, Taiwan, and Sri Lanka. It is not difficult to detect some reasons for this ability of communist elites to mobilize and organize people for sustained hard work in building a new civilization. Communist regimes have often managed to tap the enthusiasm of vast masses in fighting a foreign power or a corrupt and discredited ruling class. When such enthusiasm waned, they have not shunned coercive methods but have always backed these up with massive attempts at resocialization. Some communist parties have developed great skill in maintaining two-way lines of communication with the people at the grass roots. They have also demonstrated their ability to think and plan for the very long run. After all, they have a defined ideological aim. Finally, they are skilled in imposing order, coordination, and discipline. Foremost, revolutionary communism throughout the world has shown a remarkable ability to attract or generate great leaders. Indeed, of the men and women of the twentieth century whom future historians are likely to call "great," a substantial number were communists; let us name Luxemburg, Lenin, Trotsky, Stalin, Mao, Castro, Tito, Ho, and Giap as outstanding examples. All of them were a special mix of courage and cunning, persuasiveness, persistence, patience, and power. Often pitting themselves against overwhelming odds, they had a tremendous impact on our world.

There is irony in this, for in the eyes of Marx and Engels, the only desirable revolution was a leaderless one; they asserted that the only genuine liberation of the oppressed was their self-liberation. Moreover, the communist founding fathers' image of a better future was one of a self-governing community which could dispense with leaders, which no longer needed ruthless heroes, and in which the label of "greatness" would be reserved for outstandingly creative people in the arts and the sciences. Marxism in its original form rejected the idea of the hero in history. Therefore, when we look for great men and women with whom to compare the leaders of communism, we may find that they have most in common with the outstanding state builders of modern times, with Bismarck or Cavour and with the great captains of industry such as Henry Ford, Friedrich Krupp, John D. Rockefeller, and others—those Stalins of European and American industry who with ruthless determination transformed little machine shops and other small enterprises into huge globe-embracing industrial empires.

The great captains of industry, of course, have yielded their places to bureaucratic managers who administer complex societal machines with the help of well-established routines. Bureaucratic "rationality" has largely replaced revolutionary charisma and heroism, both in the communist world and in Western corporate enterprise. The general expectation has been that this shift would bring stability to these worlds, yet this hope has to some extent remained illusory. As this is being written, both corporate capitalism and communism seem to be in deep trouble throughout the globe. The difficulties that communism faces are very different from those now experienced in the capitalist world, although some stem from very similar causes. To this one could add that in our global political economy the problems faced by one kind of system create problems for all others also. All these complexities, however, go far beyond the scope of this book.

Some of the troubles besetting world communism today are obvious. First, there is serious division within the communist camp. Its two major powers, the USSR and the People's Republic of China, have confronted each other with profound hostility for more than two decades. Although pragmatic considerations may bring them together again for economic exchange or political co-operation, suspicion and antagonism are likely to linger in their relationship for a very long time, thus preventing genuine unity. Instead, they will continue to be very much on their guard against each other. Furthermore, the cohesion of the communist group of states is prevented by the restiveness of the USSR's European client states. In its mildest form, this shows up as a growing tendency on the part of these states to pursue a fairly independent course in political and economic relations with the noncommunist world. At its worst, it takes the form of the Polish case: This client state has become a heavy economic and political liability to the entire Soviet alliance system, and yet it would be unthinkable for Soviet policy makers to abandon it. A joke, probably originating in Eastern Europe, sums up the disunity in the communist world by referring to the Soviet Union as the only country in the world that is surrounded on all sides by hostile communist countries.

Disunity in this case is related to differences in institutions and methods of government, which in their turn can be explained by differences in cultural background, economic development, and stages in the revolution. An entirely new specialty in the social sciences, the comparative study of communist revolutions and communist systems, has been created in the Western world to study this growing heterogeneity.

Specialists in comparative communist studies disagree with each other in their assessments of the long-range prospects for global communism. The question is not only whether the countries in this group will ever be able to act as a united force, but also whether in the long run the individual systems will be viable. Some observers are respectful of the successes communist parties have had in modernizing their countries, and also believe that they are well prepared to tackle and solve the problems now facing them: economic slowdown and bureaucratic conservatism, shrinkage of resources in the face of rising expectations, sorting our priorities such as defense versus consumer interests, and coping with the many indications of tension, malaise, and unrest within their populations. Other observers stress the difficulties, some of which they view as unsurmountable, or they argue that the organizational forms and habits of rule in communist systems make them too inflexible to handle their problems successfully. However, it may be useful to remember that ever since the Russian Revolution of 1917 exaggerated claims of success and unrelieved prophesies of imminent failure have been advanced with great abandon.

The student of communist societies cannot, of course, be content merely to compare them with each other. Sooner or later, comparisons must also be made with the noncommunist world, a complicated task requiring much more work to be done. This means not only comparing communism with patterns of development in other developing countries (assessing relative successes, failures, and costs), but also making systematic comparisons between communism and corporate capitalism. Such comparisons disturb people in both the communist and the capitalist world who prefer to view these two systems as diametrically opposed to each other in ideology, institutions, and general way of life. This conviction developed during the period of deep hostility that divided the two camps in the years and decades following each of the two world wars, and in both worlds, this conviction is still strong today. Yet after Stalin's death, some writers in the West began to suggest that there was a long-range trend toward the ''convergence'' of the two systems. Capitalism, they argued, would have to increase social services and government interference in the economy, and communist societies would have to become more democratic; both would meet in some happy synthesis of democratic socialism or socialist democracy. Since then other theories of convergence have been suggested, among them the idea that technology is the force that ultimately shapes society and politics, so that as communist societies introduce modern production methods (automation, use of computers, and the like), their social structures and political institutions will have to become more similar to ours; they would then turn into welfare states and superbureaucracies. Depending on our mood, we can give such projections a benign or a threatening character. There are costs attached to the welfare state. Social scientists regard bureaucratization as the imposition of rationality on human affairs, hence as a potential blessing, but in real life the notion of imposing rationality on human relations, that is, of solving societal problems by applying the principles of engineering, may be ludicrous. We all know that bureaucracy is a problem as much as it is a solution.

In the beginning of this book I suggested a comparison between communism and revolutionary protestantism. Like contemporary communism, the Reformation began as a number of revolutionary movements, eventually erupting in a genuine revolution that ultimately established a number of Protestant states. Then followed many decades during which Protestant and Catholic states faced each other with unbridgeable hostility, and there were many international and civil wars of unprecedented ferocity. In a few corners of the world, such as Northern Ireland, these wars are still going on today. But in general, the two branches of Western Christianity have learned to coexist, and détente has been followed by collaboration and a gradual withering-away of the differences between them, or a genuinely ecumenical toleration of these differences. That was a very long process, however, and the world may no longer have time to wait for this process to occur, especially in view of the threat of nuclear annihilation. Yet, if we are very lucky, this slow process of reconciliation may also govern the long-term relationship between capitalism and communism.

Selected Readings

The literature dealing with the subject of this book is immense, even if we include only works in the English language. The following items are a relatively small selection of books that I have found interesting or useful. Of necessity, it is a somewhat haphazard selection, which includes items some other writer would have omitted and omits works which someone else would insist on including. I have listed the books according to the topics which, roughly, correspond to the principal topics covered in the book.

1. MARXISM
a. Works by Marx and Engels

Listing the many books, pamphlets, and articles by Marx and/or Engels would be tedious. So let me simply indicate that most of what they wrote is available in many relatively inexpensive editions. There are also several editions of multivolume selections and a more complete edition of their total output, under the title of *Collected Works*.

b. Biographies

W. O. Henderson, *The Life of Friedrich Engels*, 2 volumes. London, 1976.
Yvonne Kapp, *Eleanor Marx*, 2 volumes. London, 1976.
Steven Marcus, *Engels, Manchester, and the Working Class*. New York, 1974.
David McLellan, *Karl Marx*. London, 1973.
Saul K. Padover, *Karl Marx: An Intimate Biography*. New York, 1978.

c. Studies of Their Ideas

H. B. Acton, *The Illusion of the Epoch*. London, 1955.
Louis Althusser, *For Marx*. New York, 1969.
Shlomo Avineri, *The Social and Political Thought of Karl Marx*. New York, 1971.

J. F. Becker, *Marxian Political Economy*. New York, 1977.

Louis Boudin, *The Theoretical System of Karl Marx*. Chicago, 1907.

G. A. Cohen, *Karl Marx's Theory of History: A Defense*. Princeton, 1978.

Lucio Colletti, *Marxism and Hegel*. London, 1973.

Louis Dupré, *The Philosophical Foundations of Marxism*. New York, 1966.

Erich Fromm, *Marx's Concept of Man*. New York, 1969.

A. James Gregor, *A Survey of Marxism*. New York, 1965.

Eric J. Hobsbawm (ed.), *The History of Marxism. Vol. I: Marxism in Marx's Day*. Bloomington, 1982.

Richard N. Hunt, *The Political Ideas of Marx and Engels*. Vol. I. *Marxism and Totalitarian Democracy, 1818–1850*. Pittsburgh, 1974.

Leszek Kolakowski, *Main Currents of Marxism*. 3 volumes. Oxford, 1980.

Karl Korsch, *Karl Marx*. London, 1938.

George Lichtheim, *Marxism: An Historical and Critical Study*. London, 1961.

Ernest Mandel, *Marxist Economic Theory*. 2 volumes. London, 1968.

Herbert Marcuse, *Reason and Revolution*. New York, 1952.

David McLellan, *Marx before Marxism*. London, 1970.

Alfred G. Meyer, *Marxism: The Unity of Theory and Practice*. Cambridge, Mass., 1954; 2nd ed., 1970.

C. Wright Mills, *The Marxists*. New York, 1962.

Bertell Ollman, *Alienation: Marx's Conception of Man in Capitalist Society*. Cambridge, 1971.

Paul M. Sweezy, *The Theory of Capitalist Development*. New York, 1956.

Adam Ulam, *The Unfinished Revolution*. London, 1970.

Veron Venable, *Human Nature: The Marxian View*. New York, 1945.

2. MARXISM DURING THE PERIOD OF THE II. INTERNATIONAL

Evelyn Anderson, *Hammer or Anvil: The Story of the German Working Class Movement*. London, 1945.

Abraham Ascher, *Pavel Axelrod and the Development of Menshevism*. Cambridge, Mass., 1972.

Samuel H. Baron, *Plekhanov: The Father of Russian Marxism*. New York, 1963.

Max Beer, *Fifty Years of International Socialism*. London, 1935.

Eduard Bernstein, *Evolutionary Socialism*. New York, 1961.

G. D. H. Cole, *The Second International, 1889–1914*. Vol. III of *A History of Socialist Thought*. London, 1956.

Paul Frölich, *Rosa Luxemburg: Her Life and Work*. London, 1940.

Peter Gay, *The Dilemma of Democratic Socialism: Edward Bernstein's Challenge to Marx*. New York, 1962.

Israel Getzler, *Martov: A Political Biography of a Russian Social Democrat*. New York, 1967.

Richard N. Hunt, *German Social Democracy, 1918–1933*. London, 1964.

James Joll, *The Second International*. London, 1955.

J. L. H. Keep, *The Rise of Social Democracy in Russia*. Oxford, 1963.

Vernon Lidtke, *The Outlawed Party: Social Democracy in Germany, 1878–1890*. Princeton, 1966.

Rosa Luxemburg, *The Accumulation of Capital*. London, 1971.

———, *The Mass Strike, the Political Party, and the Trade Unions*. New York, 1971.

David McLellan, *Marxism After Marx*. Boston, 1979.

J. P. Nettl, *Rosa Luxemburg*. 2 volumes. Oxford, 1966.

Günter Roth, *The Social Democrats in Imperial Germany*. Totowa, N.J., 1963.

Massimo Salvadori, *Kautsky and the Socialist Revolution*. New York, 1979.

Carl E. Schorske, *German Social Democracy, 1905–1917*. Cambridge, Mass., 1955.

Z. Zeman and W. B. Schorlau, *The Merchant of Revolution: The Life of Alexander Israel Helphand*. London, 1965.

3. LENINISM

Individual books, pamphlets, and speeches by Lenin are obtainable in many inexpensive paperback editions. There are also several editions of *Selected Works*, and a 45-volume edition, in English, of his *Collected Works*.

a. Biographies

Isaac Deutscher, *Lenin's Childhood*. Oxford, 1970.

Nikolai Valentinov, *Encounters with Lenin*. Oxford, 1968.

———, *The Early Years of Lenin*. Ann Arbor, 1969.

Bertram D. Wolfe, *Three Who Made a Revolution*. New York, 1948.

b. Critical Studies

Louis Althusser, *Lenin and Philosophy*. London, 1971.

Theodore Dan, *The Origins of Bolshevism*. New York, 1964.

Leopold H. Haimson, *The Russian Marxists and the Origins of Bolshevism*. Cambridge, Mass., 1955.

Christopher Hill, *Lenin and the Russian Revolution*. London, 1947.

David Lane, *The Roots of Russian Communism*. Assen, 1969.

Moshe Lewin, *Lenin's Last Struggle*. London, 1969.

Georg Lukács, *Lenin: A Study on the Unity of His Thought*. London, 1970.

Alfred G. Meyer, *Leninism*. Cambridge, Mass., 1959.

Anton Pannekoek, *Lenin as Philosopher*. London, 1975.

Richard Pipes, *Social Democracy and the Saint Petersburg Labor Movement, 1885–1897*. Cambridge, Mass., 1963.

John P. Plamenatz, *German Marxism and Russian Communism*. London, 1954.

Arthur Rosenberg, *A History of Bolshevism*. Garden City, N.Y., 1967.

Leonard Schapiro and Peter Reddaway (eds.), *Lenin, the Man, the Theorist, the Leader*. London, 1967.

Adam Ulam, *Lenin and the Bolsheviks*. New York, 1964.

Franco Venturi, *Roots of Revolution: A History of the Populist and Socialist Movements in Nineteenth-Century Russia*. Princeton, 1960.

4. THE RUSSIAN REVOLUTION, 1917–1938

Raphael A. Abramovich, *The Soviet Revolution, 1917–1939*. London, 1962.

Arthur E. Adams (ed.), *The Russian Revolution and Bolshevik Victory: Causes and Processes*. Lexington, Mass., 1972.

Paul Avrich, *Kronstadt 1921*. Princeton, 1970.

Kendall Bailes, *Technology and Society Under Lenin and Stalin*. Princeton, 1978.

F. Beck and W. Godin, *Russian Purge and the Extraction of Confession*. New York, 1951.

Charles Bettelheim, *Class Struggles in the USSR. First Period, 1917–1923; Second Period, 1923–1930*. Hassocks, Sussex, 1977, 1978.

E. H. Carr, *The Russian Revolution from Lenin to Stalin, 1917–1929*. London, 1979.

_____, *The Bolshevik Revolution, 1917–1923*. 3 vols. London, 1950–1953.

_____, *The Interregnum, 1923–1924*. London, 1954.

_____, *Socialism in One Country, 1924–1926*. 3 vols. London, 1958–64.

William Henry Chamberlin, *The Russian Revolution, 1917–1921*. 2 vol. London, 1935.

Stephen F. Cohen, *Bukharin and the Bolshevik Revolution*. New York, 1973.

Robert Conquest, *The Great Terror*. Harmondsworth, England, 1971.

Robert V. Daniels, *The Conscience of the Revolution: Communist Opposition in Soviet Russia*. Cambridge, Mass., 1960.

_____, *Red October: The Bolshevik Revolution of 1917*. New York, 1967.

Isaac Deutscher, *The Prophet Armed: Trotsky 1879–1921*. Oxford, 1954.

_____, *The Prophet Unarmed: Trotsky 1921–1929*. Oxford, 1959.

_____, *The Prophet Outcast: Trotsky 1929–1940*. Oxford, 1963.

Alexander Erlich, *The Soviet Industrialization Debate*. Cambridge, Mass., 1960.

Merle Fainsod, *Smolensk Under Soviet Rule*. Cambridge, Mass., 1958.

Sheila Fitzpatrick, *The Commissariat of Enlightenment: Soviet Organization of Education and the Arts under Lunacharsky*. Cambridge, 1970.

_____ (ed.), *The Cultural Revolution in Russia, 1928–1931*. Bloomington, 1978.

Irving Howe, *Trotsky*. New York, 1978.

George Katkov, *The Trial of Bukharin*. London, 1969.

Baruch Knei-Paz, *The Social and Political Thought of Leon Trotsky*. Oxford, 1978.

Moshe Lewin, *Russian Peasants and Soviet Power: A Study of Collectivization*. Evanston, 1968.

Barrington Moore, Jr., *Soviet Politics: The Dilemma of Power*. Cambridge, Mass., 1950.

John Reed, *Ten Days That Shook the World*. New York, 1935.

Leonard Schapiro, *Origins of the Communist Autocracy: Political Opposition in the Soviet State. First Phase, 1917–1922*. London, 1955.

L. D. Trotsky, *The History of the Russian Revolution*. 3 vols. London, 1945.

_____, *Basic Writings*. Irving Howe, ed. London, 1964.

_____, *The Writings of Leon Trotsky, 1929–1940*. G. Breitman and S Lovell, eds. 11 vols. New York, 1972.

Robert S. Tucker and Steven F. Cohen (eds.), *The Great Purge Trial*. New York, 1965.

5. STALIN AND STALINISM

John A. Armstrong, *The Soviet Bureaucratic Elite*. New York, 1959.

Abdurakhman Avtorkhanov, *The Communist Party Apparatus*. Chicago, 1966.

Joseph S. Berliner, *Factory and Management in the USSR*. Cambridge, Mass., 1957.

Seweryn Bialer, *Stalin and His Generals*. New York, 1969.

Cyril E. Black (ed.), *The Transformation of Russian Society*. Cambridge, Mass., 1960.

Robert V. Daniels (ed.). *The Stalin Revolution—Fulfilment or Betrayal of Communism?* Boston, 1965.

Isaac Deutscher, *Stalin: A Political Biography*. Oxford, 1961.

Vera S. Dunham, *In Stalin's Time*. New York, 1976.

Merle Fainsod, *How Russia Is Ruled*. Rev. ed. Cambridge, Mass., 1963.

David Joravsky, *The Lysenko Affair*. Cambridge, Mass., 1970.

Roy A. Medvedev, *On Stalin and Stalinism*. Oxford, 1979.

Alfred G. Meyer, *The Soviet Political System*. New York, 1965.

Barrington Moore, Jr., *Terror and Progress—USSR*. Cambridge, Mass., 1954.

Olga A. Narkiewicz, *The Making of the Soviet State Apparatus*. Manchester, 1970.

Boris I. Nicolaevsky, *Power and the Soviet Elite*. New York, 1965.

Alec Nove, *Economic Reality and Soviet Politics, or Was Stalin Really Necessary?* New York, 1964.

_____, *The Soviet Economy*. New York, 1965.

_____, *Stalinism and After*. London, 1975.

Philip Selznick, *The Organizational Weapon*. New York, 1952.

Aleksandr Solzhenitsyn, *The Gulag Archipelago*. New York, 1974.

Harold Swayze, *Political Control of Literature in the USSR, 1946–1959*. Cambridge, Mass., 1962.

Robert C. Tucker, *Stalin as a Revolutionary, 1879–1929*. New York, 1973.

_____ (ed.), *Stalinism: Essays in Historical Interpretation*. New York, 1977.

Adam B. Ulam, *Stalin*. New York, 1973.

Alexander Uralov, *The Reign of Stalin*. London, 1953.

6. THE SOVIET UNION SINCE STALIN

Victor Alexandrov, *Khrushchev of the Ukraine*. New York, 1957.

John A. Armstrong, *The Politics of Totalitarianism: The Communist Party of the Soviet Union from 1934 to the Present*. New York, 1961.

Jeremy R. Azrael, *Managerial Power and Soviet Politics*. Cambridge, Mass., 1966.

Donald D. Barry and Carol Barner-Barry, *Contemporary Soviet Politics: An Introduction*. Englewood Cliffs, N.J., 1978.

Joseph S. Berliner, *The Innovation Decision in Soviet Industry*. Cambridge, Mass., 1978.

George Breslauer, *Five Images of the Soviet Future*. Berkeley, 1978.

_____, *Khrushchev and Brezhnev as Leaders: Building Authority in Soviet Politics*. London, 1982.

T. Cliff, *State Capitalism in Russia*. London, 1974.

William J. Conyngham, *Industrial Management in the Soviet Union*. Stanford, 1973.

E. Crankshaw, *Khrushchev*. London, 1966.

Alexander Dallin and Thomas Larson, *Soviet Politics Since Khrushchev*. Englewood Cliffs, N.J., 1968.

Maurice Dobb, *Soviet Economic Development Since 1917*. New York, 1966.

John Dornberg, *Brezhnev, The Masks of Power*. New York, 1974.

George Fischer, *The Soviet System and Modern Society*. New York, 1968.

Sheila Fitzpatrick, *Education and Social Mobility in the USSR*. London, 1979.

Theodore Friedgut, *Political Participation in the USSR*. Princeton, 1979.

David Granick, *The Red Executive*. Garden City, N.Y., 1960.

Thane Gustafson, *Reform in Soviet Politics*. New York, 1981.

Werner G. Hahn, *The Politics of Soviet Agriculture*. Baltimore, 1972.

Mark W. Hopkins, *Mass Media in the Soviet Union*. New York, 1970.

Jerry F. Hough, *The Soviet Prefects: The Local Party Organs in Industrial Decision-Making*. Cambridge, Mass., 1969.

_____, *The Soviet Union and Social Science Theory*. Cambridge, Mass., 1977.

_____, *Soviet Leadership in Transition*. Washington, 1980.

_____, and Merle Fainsod, *How the Soviet Union Is Governed.* Cambridge, Mass., 1979.

A. Katsenellenboigen, *Studies in Soviet Economic Planning.* White Plains, N.Y., 1978.

David Lane, *The Socialist Industrial State.* London, 1976.

Wolfgang Leonard, *The Kremlin Since Stalin.* Oxford, 1962.

Borys Levytsky, *The Soviet Political Elite.* Stanford, 1970.

Carl A. Linden, *Khrushchev and the Soviet Leadership, 1957–1964.* Baltimore, 1966.

Roy and Zhores Medvedev, *Khrushchev: The Years in Power.* New York, 1977.

Alec Nove, *An Economic History of the USSR.* London, 1969.

_____, *Political Economy and Soviet Socialism.* London, 1978.

Robert J. Osborn, *Soviet Social Policies: Welfare, Equality, and Community* Homewood, Ill., 1970.

T. H. Rigby, *Communist Party Membership in the USSR.* Princeton, 1968

Myron Rush, *The Rise of Khrushchev.* Washington, 1958.

_____, *Political Succession in the USSR.* New York, 1965.

Karl Ryavec, *Implementation of Soviet Economic Reforms.* New York, 1975.

Nicholas Spulber, *Soviet Strategy for Economic Growth.* Bloomington, 1964.

Michel Tatu, *Power in the Kremlin from Khrushchev to Kosygin.* New York, 1970.

Alexander Yanov, *The Russian New Right.* Berkeley, 1978.

Murray Yanowitch and Wesley A. Fisher (eds.), *Social Stratification and Mobility in the USSR.* White Plains, N.Y., 1973.

7. SOVIET IDEOLOGY

Nikolai Bukharin and Evgeni Preobrazhenski, *The ABC of Communism.* London, 1924.

Fundamentals of Marxism-Leninism. Moscow, 1958.

Jerome Gilison, *The Soviet Image of Utopia.* Baltimore, 1975.

Loren R. Graham, *Science and Philosophy in the Soviet Union.* New York, 1966.

Alex Inkeles, *Public Opinion in Soviet Russia.* Cambridge, Mass., 1950.

David Joravsky, *Soviet Marxism and Natural Science.* London, 1961.

Wolfgang Leonard, *Three Faces of Marxism.* New York, 1974.

Herbert Marcuse, *Soviet Marxism.* New York, 1958.

Ellen Propper Mickiewicz, *Soviet Political Schools.* New Haven, 1967.

John Somerville, *Soviet Philosophy.* New York, 1946.

Rudolf L. Tökes (ed.), *Dissent in the USSR: Politics, Ideology, and People.* Baltimore, 1977.

Gustav A. Wetter, S.J., *Dialectical Materialism: A Historical and Semantic Survey of Philosophy in the Soviet Union.* London, 1958.

_____, *Soviet Ideology Today*. New York, 1966.

8. THE COMMUNIST INTERNATIONAL, 1919–1943

Branz Borkenau, *World Communism*. Ann Arbor, 1962.

Jane Degras (ed.), *The Communist International, 1919–1943*. 2 vols. Oxford, 1956–1965.

Marian Kamil Dziewanowski, *The Communist Party of Poland*. Cambridge, Mass., 1959.

Louis Fischer, *The Soviets in World Affairs*. New York, 1960.

Ruth Fischer, *Stalin and German Communism*. Cambridge, Mass., 1948.

Helmut Gruber (ed.), *International Communism in the Era of Lenin: A Documentary History*. Garden City, N.Y., 1972.

Gustav Hilger and Alfred G. Meyer, *The Incompatible Allies: A Memoir-History of German-Soviet Relations, 1919–1941*. New York, 1953.

Branco Lazitch and Milorad Drachkovitch, *Lenin and the Comintern*. Stanford, 1972.

Kermit E. McKenzie, *Comintern and World Revolution, 1928–1943*. New York, 1964.

D. W. Morgan, *The Socialist Left and the German Revolution: A History of the German Independent Social Democratic Party, 1917–1922*. Ithaca, N.Y., 1975.

Olga A. Narkiewicz, *Marxism and the Reality of Power, 1919–1980*. New York, 1981.

Alfred J. Rieber, *Stalin and the French Communist Party, 1941–1947*. New York, 1962.

Hugh Seton-Watson, *From Lenin to Khrushchev: The History of World Communism*. New York, 1960.

R. Tiersky, *French Communism, 1920–1972*. New York, 1974.

Alan S. Whiting, *Soviet Policies in China, 1917–1924*. New York, 1954.

9. THE SOVIET UNION IN WORLD AFFAIRS

Alexander Dallin (ed.), *Soviet Conduct in World Affairs*. New York, 1960.

Erik P. Hoffman and Frederick J. Fleron (eds.), *The Conduct of Soviet Foreign Policy*. Chicago, 1971.

J. Malcolm Mackintosh, *Strategy and Tactics of Soviet Foreign Policy*. New York, 1963.

Alvin Z. Rubinstein (ed.), *The Foreign Policy of the Soviet Union*. New York, 1972.

William Zimmerman, *Soviet Perspectives on International Relations, 1956–1967*. Princeton, 1969.

10. THIRD WORLD COMMUNISM—GENERAL

Samir Amin, *Imperialism and Unequal Development*. Hassocks, Sussex, 1978.

Paul Baran, *The Political Economy of Growth*, New York, 1957.

Amilcar Cabral, *Return to the Source*. New York, 1969.

———, *Unity and Struggle*. New York, 1973.

Gérard Chaliand, *Revolutions in the Third World from 1945 to the Present*. Hassocks, Sussex, 1977.

David Horowitz, *Imperialism and Revolution*. New York, 1971.

Roger E. Kanet, *The Soviet Union and the Developing Countries*. Baltimore, 1974.

John H. Kautsky, *Communism and the Politics of Development*. New York, 1968.

Robert Scalapino (ed.), *Communist Revolution in Asia*. Englewood Cliffs, N.J., 1965.

Immanuel M. Wallerstein, *The Capitalist World Economy*. New York, 1979.

Eric R. Wolf, *Peasant Wars of the Twentieth Century*. New York, 1969.

11. COMMUNISM IN CHINA

A. Doak Barnett, *Uncertain Passage: China's Transition to the Post-Mao Era*. Washington, 1974.

Richard Baum, *Prelude to Revolution: Mao, the Party, and the Peasant Question, 1962–1966*. New York, 1975.

———, (ed.), *China in Torment*. Englewood Cliffs, N.J., 1971.

Lucien Bianco, *Origins of the Chinese Revolution, 1915–1949*. Stanford, 1971.

Conrad Brandt, *Stalin's Failure in China*. Cambridge, Mass., 1958.

———, B. I. Schwartz, and J. K. Fairbank, *A Documentary History of Chinese Communism*. Cambridge, Mass., 1952.

P. H. Chang, *Radicals and Radical Ideology in China's Cultural Revolution*. New York, 1973.

C. L. Chiou, *Maoism in Action: The Cultural Revolution*. New York, 1974.

Arthur A. Cohen, *The Communism of Mao Tse-tung*. Chicago, 1964.

Lowell Dittmer, *Liu Shao-chi and the Chinese Cultural Revolution*. Berkeley, 1974.

Alexander Eckstein, *China's Economic Development: The Interplay of Scarcity and Ideology*. Ann Arbor, 1975.

C. P. Fitzgerald, *The Birth of Communist China*. London, 1964.

———, *Mao Tse-tung and China*. London, 1977.

William Hinton, *Fanshen*. New York, 1966.

———, *Hundred Day War: The Cultural Revolution at Tsinghua University*. New York, 1972.

———, *Turning Point in China: An Essay on the Cultural Revolution*. New York, 1972.

Harold Isaacs, *The Tragedy of the Chinese Revolution*. London, 1938.

Chalmers A. Johnson, *Peasant Nationalism and Communist Power: The Emergence of Revolutionary China, 1937–1945*. Stanford, 1953.

———, *Ideology and Politics in Contemporary China*. Seattle, 1973.

K. S. Karol, *The Second Chinese Revolution*. London, 1975.

Roderick MacFarquhar (ed.), *China Under Mao*. Cambridge, Mass., 1966.

Mao Tse-tung, *Selected Works*, 5 vols. Peking, 1965–1977.

Maurice Meisner, *Mao's China*. New York, 1977.

Robert C. North, *Moscow and the Chinese Communists*. Stanford, 1953.

Joan Robinson, *The Cultural Revolution in China*. London, 1969.

Thomas W. Robinson (ed.), *The Cultural Revolution in China*. Berkeley, 1971.

Stuart Schram, *Mao Tse-tung*. Harmondsworth, 1966.

———, (ed.), *Authority, Participation, and Cultural Change in China*. Cambridge, 1973.

Franz Schurmann, *Ideology and Organization in Communist China*. Berkeley, 1966.

Benjamin I. Schwartz, *Chinese Communism and the Rise of Mao*. Cambridge, Mass., 1951.

Mark Selden, *The Yenan Way in Revolutionary China*. Cambridge, Mass., 1972.

Edgar Snow, *The Long Revolution*. New York, 1971.

Richard H. Solomon, *Mao's Revolution and the Chinese Political Culture*. Berkeley, 1971.

James R. Townsend, *Politics in China*. Boston, 1980.

Ezra Vogel, *Canton Under Communism: Programs and Politics in a Provincial Capital, 1949–1968*. New York, 1969.

Donald Zagoria, *The Sino-Soviet Conflict, 1956–1961*. Princeton, 1962.

12. VIET NAM

Bernard Fall, *The Two Vietnams*. New York, 1967.

Frances Fitzgerald, *Fire in the Lake*. Boston, 1972.

David Halberstam, *Ho*. New York, 1971.

Jean Lacouture, *Ho Chi Minh: A Political Biography*. New York, 1968.

Robert F. Turner, *Vietnamese Communism: Its Origins and Development*. Stanford, 1975.

Alexander B. Woodside, *Community and Revolution in Modern Vietnam*. Boston, 1976.

13. COMMUNISM IN LATIN AMERICA

L. A. Anguilar, *Marxism in Latin America*. New York, 1968.

R. Bonachea and N. P. Valdes (eds.), *Cuba in Revolution*. New York, 1972.

Fidel Castro, *Selected Works*. R. Bonachea and N. P. Valdes (eds.). 3 vols. Cambridge, Mass., 1972.

Regis Debray, *Revolution in the Revolution?* New York, 1967.

Richard R. Fagen, *The Transformation of Political Culture in Cuba*. Stanford, 1968.

Andrew Gunder Frank, *Capitalism and Underdevelopment in Latin America*. New York, 1969.

Ernesto "Che" Guevara, *Guerrilla Warfare*. New York, 1961.

Maurice Halperin, *The Rise and Decline of Fidel Castro*. Berkeley, 1972.

Leo Huberman and Paul M. Sweezy, *Socialism in Cuba*. New York, 1969.

K. S. Karol, *Guerrillas in Power: The Course of the Cuban Revolution*. New York, 1970.

Lee Lockwood, *Castro's Cuba, Cuba's Fidel*. New York, 1971.

Michel Lowy, *The Marxism of Che Guevara*. New York, 1973.

Herbert L. Matthews, *Castro: A Political Biography*. New York, 1961.

_____, *The Cuban Story*. New York, 1961.

James O'Connor, *The Origins of Socialism in Cuba*. Ithaca, N.Y., 1970.

Ronald Radosh (ed.), *The New Cuba: Paradoxes and Potentials*. New York, 1976.

Andres Suarez, *Cuba: Castro and Communism*. Cambridge, 1967.

Hugh Thomas, *Cuba: The Pursuit of Freedom*. New York, 1971.

14. COMMUNISM IN EASTERN EUROPE

Thomas A. Baylis, *The Technical Intelligentsia and the East German Elite*. Berkeley, 1974.

Zbigniew K. Brzezinski, *The Soviet Bloc: Unity and Conflict*. Cambridge, Mass., 1967.

D. Childs, *East Germany*. London, 1969.

Bogoslav Dobrin, *Bulgarian Economic Development Since World War II*. New York, 1975.

Francois Fejto, *A History of the People's Democracies: Eastern Europe Since Stalin*. New York, 1971.

Charles Gati (ed.), *The Politics of Modernization in Eastern Europe*. New York, 1975.

P. Hare, H. Radice, and N. Swain (eds.), *Hungary: A Decade of Economic Reform*. London, 1981.

Chris Harman, *Bureaucracy and Revolution in Eastern Europe*. London, 1974.

Ghita Ionescu, *The Politics of the Eastern Communist States*. London, 1967.

Andrew C. Janos (ed.), *Authoritarian Politics in Communist Europe*. Berkeley, 1976.

Kenneth Jowitt, *Revolutionary Breakthroughs and National Development.* Berkeley, 1971.

Teresa Kakowska-Harmstone and Andrew György (eds.), *Communism in Eastern Europe.* Bloomington, 1979.

Heinz Lippman, *Honecker and the New Politics of Europe.* New York, 1972.

Emil Loebl, *Sentenced and Tried: The Stalinist Purges in Czechoslovakia.* London, 1969.

Ramadan Marmullaku, *Albania and the Albanians.* London, 1975.

M. McCauley, *Marxism-Leninism in the German Democratic Republic.* London, 1979.

Nissan Oren, *Bulgarian Communism.* New York, 1971.

_____ *Revolution Administered: Agrarianism and Communism in Bulgaria.* Baltimore, 1973.

Jiři Pelikan, *The Czechoslovak Purge Trials, 1950–1954.* London, 1971.

Ota Sik, *Czechoslovakia: The Bureaucratic Economy.* White Plains, N.Y., 1972.

H. Gordon Skilling, *The Governments of Communist East Europe.* New York, 1966.

Richard F. Starr, *Communist Regimes in Eastern Europe.* Stanford, 1977.

K. E. Wädekin, *Agrarian Policies in Communist Europe: A Critical Introduction.* Totowa, N.J., 1982.

Paul E. Zinner (ed.), *National Communism and Popular Revolt in Eastern Europe.* New York, 1956.

15. YUGOSLAVIA

George W. Hoffman and Fred W. Neal, *Yugoslavia and the New Communism.* New York, 1962.

Branco Horvat, *The Yugoslav Economic System.* White Plains, N.Y., 1976.

_____, Mihajlo Marković, Rudi Supek, and H. Kramer (eds.), *Self-Governing Socialism: A Reader.* 2 vols. New York, 1975.

Mihajlo Marković and Robert S. Cohen, *Yugoslavia: The Rise and Fall of Socialist Humanism.* Nottingham, 1975.

Gajo Petrović, *Marx in the Mid-Twentieth Century.* New York, 1967.

Dennison Rusinow, *The Yugoslav Experiment, 1948–1974.* Berkeley, 1977.

Gerson S. Sher, *Praxis: Marxist Criticism and Dissent in Socialist Yugoslavia.* Bloomington, 1977.

Svetozar Stojanovic, *Between Ideals and Reality: A Critique of Socialism and Its Future.* New York, 1973.

Adam B. Ulam, *Titoism and the Cominform.* Cambridge, Mass., 1951.

Sharon Zukin, *Beyond Marx and Tito: Theory and Practice in Yugoslavia.* New York, 1975.

16. COMMUNIST HERESIES IN EASTERN EUROPE

Rudolf Bahro, *The Alternative in East Europe.* New York, 1973.

Zygmunt Bauman, *Socialism, The Active Utopia.* London, 1976.

Felipe García Casals, *The Syncretic Society.* White Plains, N.Y. 1980.

Richard T. De George, *The New Marxism: Soviet and East European Marxism Since 1956.* New York, 1968.

Galia Golan, *The Czechoslovak Reform Movement: Communism in Crisis, 1926–1968.* New York, 1971.

Andras Hegedüs, *Socialism and Bureaucracy.* London, 1976.

Zbigniew Jordan, *Philosophy and Ideology: The Development of Philosophy and Marxism-Leninism in Poland Since the Second World War.* Dordrecht, 1963.

Leszek Kolakowski, *Marxism and Beyond.* London, 1968.

György Konrad and Ivan Szeleny, *The Intellectuals on the Road to Class Power.* New York, 1979.

Karel Kosik, *Dialectics of the Concrete.* Dordrecht, 1976.

Vladimir Kusin, *The Intellectual Origins of the Prague Spring: The Development of Reformist Ideas in Czechoslovakia, 1956–1967.* Cambridge, 1971.

Eugen Loebl, *My Mind on Trial.* New York, 1976.

Roy A. Medvedev, *On Socialist Democracy.* New York, 1975.

Jiři Pelikan, *The Secret Vysocany Congress of the Czech Communist Party.* New York, 1971.

_____, *Socialist Opposition in Eastern Europe.* London, 1976.

Marc Rakovski, *Towards an East European Marxism.* New York, 1978.

Adam Schaff, *Marxism and the Human Individual.* New York, 1970.

Ota Šik, *The Third Way.* London, 1976.

Z. A. B. Zeman, *Prague Spring.* New York, 1969.

17. EUROCOMMUNISM AND RELATED TOPICS

Carl Boggs and D. Plotke (eds.), *The Politics of Eurocommunism.* London, 1980.

Santiago Carrillo, *Dialogue on Spain.* London, 1975.

_____, *Eurocommunism and the State.* London, 1977.

F. Claudin, *Eurocommunism and Socialism.* New York, 1978.

Regis Debray, *Conversations with Allende.* London, 1972.

G. Fiori, *Antonio Gramsci: Life of a Revolutionary.* New York, 1973.

Erich Fromm (ed.), *Socialist Humanism.* Garden City, N.Y., 1966.

R. Godson and S. Haseler (eds.), *Eurocommunism.* New York, 1978.

James Joll, *Gramsci.* London, 1977.

D. G. Kousoulas, *Revolution and Defeat: The Story of the Greek Communist Party.* Oxford, 1965.

George Lichtheim, *Lukács*. London, 1970.
George Lukács, *History and Class Consciousness*. London, 1971.
Ernest Mandel, *From Stalinism to Eurocommunism*. London, 1978.
M. Reptis, *Revolution and Counterrevolution in Chile*. London, 1974.

18. THE COMPARATIVE STUDY OF COMMUNIST SYSTEMS

Archie Brown and Jack Gray (eds.), *Political Culture and Political Change in Communist States*. London, 1979.
Leonard J. Cohan and Jane P. Shapiro (eds.), *Communist Systems in Comparative Perspective*. Garden City, N.Y., 1974.
Chalmers A. Johnson (ed.)., *Change in Communist Systems*. Stanford, 1970.
Barrington Moore, Jr., *Social Origins of Dictatorship and Democracy*. Boston, 1967.
Donald W. Treadgold (ed.), *Soviet and Chinese Communism: Similarities and Differences*. Seattle, 1967.
Robert G. Wesson, *Communism and Communist Systems*. Englewood Cliffs, N.J., 1978.

Index

ABOUT THE AUTHOR

Alfred G. Meyer was born in Germany, emigrated to the United States in 1939, and served in the U. S. Army 1941–1945. His MA (Slavic languages and literature) and Ph.D. (political science) are from Harvard. He has taught at Harvard, the University of Washington, and Michigan State University, and since 1966 has been professor of political science at the University of Michigan. He has held various administrative appointments in academic research and has been awarded fellowships from the Ford, Rockefeller, and Guggenheim foundations. He has also received recognition for outstanding performance as a teacher and counselor. His books have been translated into French, Italian, German, Spanish, and Korean. They include *The Incompatible Allies* (with Gustav Hilger); *Marxism: The Unity of Theory and Practice; Leninism;* and *The Soviet Political System*. Professor Meyer has recently been working on a study of Lily Braun, a German feminist and socialist.